Cat Talk

Other books by Carole C. Wilbourn:

THE INNER CAT

CATS PREFER IT THIS WAY

CATS ON THE COUCH

Cat Talk

WHAT YOUR CAT
IS TRYING
TO TELL YOU

Carole C. Wilbourn
CAT THERAPIST

Illustrated by Jane Chambless-Rigie

PUBLISHERS CHOICE
NEW YORK

A PUBLISHERS CHOICE BOOK

Originally published in 1979 by Macmillan Publishing Co., Inc.

Publishers Choice revised trade edition published 1991

Copyright ©1979, 1991 by Carole C. Wilbourn

Cover photograph by Ed Haas
Cover design by Neuwirth & Associates, Inc.

Publishers Choice is a registered trademark and imprint of National Syndications, Inc.
230 Fifth Avenue
New York, NY 10001

ISBN 1-879955-00-8

10 9

Printed in the U.S.A.

In loving memory of my parents.

For Hugh MacCraig, who told me I must write about cats.

For Phyllis Levy, who believed this book must be.

For my two guys, Sunny-Blue and Ziggy-Star-Dust, who support my inner force.

And on behalf of Tyrone Power and all the other lonely cats.

CONTENTS

Cat Talk

INTRODUCTION:
WHAT IS A CAT THERAPIST?

Quite often I am asked what a cat therapist is and what a cat therapist does. I explain that I try to help people understand their cat's day-to-day needs, so that person and cat can relate in a way that promotes the emotional and physical health of both. However, many of my cases involve cats who have already developed emotional problems. Emotional problems often trigger medical ones. That's why I feel it so important to treat the *total cat*.

The other most commonly asked questions are, "How did you become a cat therapist? Is there a special school?" The second question is easier to answer. No, there is no special school. The answer to the first question is more complex and begins in Los Angeles in 1969, when I was visiting my sister, Gail. Gail asked me what I would want if my special career wish could be granted.

"I want to help cats!"

I was living in New York at this time, involved in various cat charities and receiving my income from teaching high school and working weekends as a bunny at the New York Playboy Club. But cats were always on my mind. A happy cat made me a happy person.

One year later, my goal was still only a dream. I had separated from my first husband, but I had kept our two cats, Oliver and Sambo. I took a friend's sick cat to my local vet. There I met

Paul Rowan, his associate. "Met" is too mild a word for that experience! Paul knocked me for a loop. We fell in love. So, Paul joined cats as the other constant in my life. Most of my free time was spent with cats or with Paul, but I kept trying to include both cats *and* Paul so neither passion would be neglected. Since my cat passion was contagious, soon after it seemed very natural for the two of us to devote our leisure time to taking care of cats.

In 1971 I had my first "professional" experience. We were living in Malibu and had opened an emergency veterinary service nearby. Two years later, we returned to New York and were both involved in various other veterinary practices. At the time I was taking postgraduate courses in psychology. I spent much of my time observing cats' behavior. From their actions I deduced their emotions and interpreted their feelings. I found that if a cat's emotions were well balanced, so was his behavior. Conversely, if he felt badly, he would have behavioral changes.

In 1973, Paul and I opened The Cat Practice in New York's West Village. I named it The Cat Practice because we wanted it to become a cat's utopia, where a cat could receive the care and understanding he needed and deserved. It was the first hospital in New York City and surrounding area devoted exclusively to cats. Now, at last, I had the chance to develop a practice devoted exclusively to cats. My dream was to create an ideal environment into which people could feel happy and comfortable bringing their cats. I believed that the more relaxed the cat's person was, the easier it would be for his cat to also relax.

The office, which was only a few blocks from our home, was on the third floor of an old carriage house. Since our clients had to stagger up two flights of stairs with one or more cat carriers, I decorated the stairway with composites of cat photos with captions under each picture to provide a scenic ascent. Looking at cats always makes cat people feel good. Once cats get under your skin, there's no chance of them letting you go.

We decorated the waiting room with comfortable wicker chairs complete with gaily colored cushions, plants, a splendid cat and horse (in honor of Capers, our horse in Malibu) mural, and a large bulletin board. The bulletin board quickly filled with cards and letters written in reply to our resident cats' letters and cards. While waiting for their appointment, clients spent their time here, either relating or listening to another cat's story.

From the waiting room, the cat and his person entered the exam room—a spacious, sunny room with a large skylight. Paul designed his own cabinets and exam table; these were modular units made of wood. No stainless steel or formica! Since the cabinets were modular, we could change the room arrangement at will.

A patient never left empty-pawed. Each was given a catnip toy made by our staff. At first, we used a toy sewing machine from F.A.O. Schwartz to make them, but it wasn't rugged enough to keep up with our large volume, so we switched to an adult model. The Fabric Shop nearby, whose owners are cat-oriented, supplied us with scraps to make the toys, which were in the shape of cat faces, suns, and fish. Because people always remarked, "What's this?" the toys became known as "whatsies." Not only did each patient receive a toy, but he also received a cheer-up card in the mail. Occasionally a client would call and ask to speak to the person who had signed the card. One of our staff would then explain that the signer was a resident *cat* and not a *person*.

If a cat were sick and had to be hospitalized or needed surgery, he was admitted to the nursery. This was my pride and joy! Since the room had a southern exposure, we filled the windows with hanging plants and adorned the walls with colorful pictures. Each patient was admitted to a wooden cubicle with an upper berth to sleep on, a light to keep him warm, and a pane of glass in the door so that he could see out. There were soft, clean towels for comfort, a litterbox, and a blanket if the patient were cold. Each cubicle was individually air vented, and the air filtered out the window to prevent cross-infection. I called the cubicles "nooks" instead of the usual name "cages," which creates such gloomy images. I had the nurses spray the nooks with perfume to freshen the air from litterbox odors and because cats are attracted to pleasant scents. When our perfume supply dwindled, our clients generously contributed their extra bottles of perfume. As time went on, we added another adjoining nursery. This time, the nooks were circular instead of square, and there was even a suite for companion cats. It was quite a moment when the first client requested the suite for her cat, Crusader, a real chunker.

I used a private room in the back of the hospital for patients that needed rest and complete isolation. I named it the John Galt Sanctuary after one of my intensive care patients. Vanessa, John's first private nurse, had covered one wall with a mural of cats at the beach.

The practice started slowly. During the first several months, I was able to answer the phone and assist Paul with his appointments and surgery. We wanted things to move slowly and smoothly so our foundation would be solid and well built. Our routine had to be tight so the procedures could be taught easily. When things became so busy that I could no longer cover all of the various positions, I hired and trained people (mostly college students) to take over portions of my duties. I divided the jobs into shifts so that no one person could become too saturated. Only cheerful and fresh people can clearly communicate comforting messages to patients and clients.

One of my chief goals was to convey to each person the importance of being relaxed and low key with the patients. Because a cat is so sensitive to feelings, a person's anxious-energy level would only add to a patient's discomfort. During training, I taught assistants how to distract both the patient and client when Paul had to give an injection. If the cat and his person's attention were distracted, the pain and discomfort were minimal.

I now spent most of my time in the nursery. I knew it was essential that I understand how each patient was feeling. I interpreted this through his breathing, facial expression, and body posture. I passed my recommendations on to Paul, who would combine them with his knowledge and diagnostic tools. At times, I could recognize what was wrong with a patient faster with my skills than Paul could with his. Each day when appointments were finished, we would confer about those cases that were emotionally oriented and other cases on which he thought I could shed light.

We provided nursing care from 7:00 A.M. until 9:00 P.M.; but I couldn't rest easy during the night if stressed or terminal patients were uncomfortable. Many times I would run over to the hospital in the middle of the night to cuddle a patient. When we were able to afford a nurse who was on duty until the wee hours of the morning, I developed peace of mind and dubbed the shift "the late-late show."

As time went on, I realized that we needed a special recovery nurse to stay with patients recovering from anesthesia. Barney, who had just retired from her business, happily joined the staff. I knew that Barney's strong will and courage had allowed her former cat, Charlie My Boy, an epileptic, to live a happy and comfortable life longer than anyone could have predicted. And Barney's innate understanding of plants was an unexpected bonus.

The Cat Practice staff now consisted of college students; Sondra, an international airline stewardess; high school students; Barney, our "senior citizen"; and even preadolescents. I realized we needed a kid's touch when a cat named Spencer Tracy recovered from a severe urinary problem but was so sad and blue that he refused to eat and wouldn't respond to contact. His heart seemed to yearn for the little girl he used to live with. I arranged for Simone, a ten-year-old girl who lived next door, to come by after school. She brought along Selina and Liz, her school chums. Each afternoon they'd sign Spencer's visitor list and he'd purr and melt as they stroked and cuddled him. Spencer's appetite perked up and his eyes glowed. Thanks to "les Jeunes Filles Auxiliary," as they were called, Spencer rallied, was

7

adopted, and went to live with Thai Thai, who also needed her own cat to love.

All our patients thrived on the comforting and positive support they received from our staff. We also encouraged people to visit their cats while they were hospitalized. I remember from my own hospital stays how visitors cheered me and the important part the nursing staff played. Once, as I was being wheeled into the operating room, a nurse grabbed my hand and squeezed it to give me support. It felt wonderful. The visitors often brought special treats for their cats and delectable goodies or plants for the staff. One client arrived unexpectedly one evening with a dozen pies from a local bakery, in honor of his cat, Black Cat. Another client made a stained glass window with The Cat Practice written on it, which was hung in the waiting room window.

As time passed, Paul and I realized how instrumental my observations and opinions were in dealing with cases. Instead of trying to pass my information through Paul, I began private consultations with the person and his cat. I could often spot various reactions that I'd experienced with former patients and speed the diagnosis. I held my consultation in a quiet, sunny room at the back of the hospital. I decorated it like our little house in Malibu and named it the Private Beach. The room was constructed of rough pine, with a shiplike porthole that looked in on the adjoining area. Every person and cat enjoyed a warm and relaxing reaction to the environment, especially in the daytime when the sun came shining through the windows. I loved watching each cat relax in his opened carrier or on his person's lap as we discussed his case history, and he felt the helpful energy around him. Imagine the cat's relief when he realized I was just going to stroke and observe him, and nothing more! As The Practice evolved, Paul and I saw each new case together so we would have a complete history of each patient.

In October 1978, Paul and I sold The Cat Practice to Dr.

Skip Sullivan, who had worked with us while attending veterinary school.

To become a cat therapist, I recommend the following:

1. Find a sympathetic veterinarian with whom you can establish a trustful relationship.

2. Design a health-inducing and aesthetically pleasing environment for work.

3. Constantly observe, and never hide from, even painful or unpopular conclusions.

4. Make sure your clients understand your recommendations.

5. Test, retest, and change your theories when necessary.

Since I've left The Practice, I have more time to write and devote to my individual cases. Cats have given me a better understanding of real dignity, pride, and perseverance. I hope to continue to add to their nurturing. I've written this book for you, to help you interpret your cat's body language and to explain how I go about interpreting a cat's more subtle communications. I hope it will enable you to understand your "cat's talk."

POSTSCRIPT

It makes me so very happy that Cat Talk, *which I wrote 13 years ago, is once more in print. I think you will find that I speak directly "for" cats and what I've written about cats' behavior still applies. Perhaps it is even more timely now because the cat is now the number-one household pet. So many inaccurate conceptions about cats have been refuted in the past several years. Consequently,* Cat Talk *now has even a larger and more receptive audience.*

Now my cat practice consists primarily of house calls. My longest distance house call was to Maui. My patient, Pokane, was positive for feline leukemia; glaucoma was her primary symptom. Her care-givers had engaged me on a phone-and-letter consultation basis to improve the quality of Pokane's life. But when Boots, Pokane's companion, began to ambush her out of frustration, and an indigent, needy tomcat they dubbed Schwartzie set up residence in their driveway—and their move to a new house was imminent—they requested a house call. It was indeed a coup! Several sessions improved Pokane and Boots' relationship and I devised a program to integrate Schwartzie into their new household with the minimum of stress. The move was a success and Schwartzie, the former "tomcat," settled into his new domestic status with uncanny ease.

My phone-and-letter consultations have reached as far as Australia and Turkey. I derive such great fulfillment when I can take the mystery out of a cat's seemingly deviant behavior. My column for Cat Fancy *magazine, "Cats on the Couch," is the ideal remedy for this. I make it a practice to respond to each letter I receive even if I don't choose to include it in my column. If a person cares enough to contact me with a cat problem, I'll certainly reply.*

I've started to teach classes on cat behavior for The Learning Annex. Most of my classes are in Manhattan but my itinerary has included Washington D.C., Philadelphia, Los Angeles and San Diego. Cats are such a popular phenomena that "Dear T'abbe" is a new column I've been asked to write for The Learning Annex *magazine.*

My marital split with the veterinarian, Paul Rowan, in 1982, with whom I worked, led to an increase in the volume of my cat practice. Many of my case referrals are from veterinarians.

I later became part of the advisory board at The Humane Society of New York. In 1988 I gave them the rights to my book Cats on the Couch *and all the proceeds go to the animals. The first place to carry my book in Manhattan was Paw n' Claw, an animal supply shop in Greenwich Village, New York. Other places now include Lick Your Chops, Creature Features, Whiskers, Pet Stop and the boutiques The Cat Store and Just Cats. In Philadelphia my book is sold at a shop called The Black Cat. It is also available by mail order from Felix, a company in Seattle, Washington.*

Many of my case referrals are from veterinarians, the first of whom were Drs. Paul Cavanagh and Ann Lucas. In 1987 Drs. Paul Cavanagh and Stuart Brodsky asked me to join their staff at Westside Veterinary Center where I see patients and give consultations. We work together to devise "total" treatment programs that meet the needs of animals with

10

both psychologically and physiologically based disorders. But a large part of my agenda at Westside is to offer preventive therapy which can nip a cat problem in the bud.

Dr. Lewis Berman of Park East Animal Hospital is another source of my case referrals. He's done much to foster the proper intensive care of cats. I also work with Dr. Sally Haddock and her associates of St. Mark's Veterinary Hospital. My working relationship with Dr. Ann Lucas and her associates has now reached its ninth year. I've also started to work in conjunction with Dr. Gene Solomon and Paul Schwartz of the newly opened Center for Veterinary Care. It's not unusual for me to receive veterinarians' referrals from nearby boroughs and even from across the country.

Although I work on a formal basis with The Humane Society of New York, I also work informally with The A.S.P.C.A. departments of education and adoption. I have also lectured at the Animal Medical Center in Manhattan on cat behavior.

Because of my unusual expertise, I receive an enormous amount of international media coverage. I recently taped television shows for England and Germany and there was a feature print story about me in You, *the Sunday supplement of the* London Mail. *My work was also included in a Japanese television documentary.*

The two cats in my life are now Sunny-Blue and Ziggy-Star-Dust. Sunny was an indigent Chocolate Point Siamese who was found in Harlem in 1979. Paul Rowan and I adopted him for our cat Muggsy-Baggins after the demise of our beloved Sambo. Sunny turned out to be an attack cat sparked by the tomcat and abandonment syndromes. Baggins and Paul were his key tension targets. He was, fortunately, another of my success stories and quickly recovered, bonding beautifully with Baggins and graciously accepting Paul. Sunny and Baggins' relationship was brief. Baggins joined his Sam a year later. We eventually adopted Honey-Blue, a lithe, tortoise-shell kitten for Sunny. But two years later Paul and I divorced and it was best for her *to join Paul. Several months later I adopted Ziggy-Star-Dust, a young black kitten, from a trendy Japanese restaurant, where he had lived since being found in the East Village. He is the absolute antithesis of Sunny. While Sunny craves people's attention,*

11

Star-Dust is a cat-oriented being. Sunny is his main object of affection. This suits Sunny to a T.

Because Sunny has such a need for recognition, he joins me on many of my television appearances which have included "Regis and Kathie Lee" and Channel Thirteen's Telethon. He adores the camera and is a ready and willing subject. He has also participated in inter-species therapy at nursing homes and Marble Collegiate Church. He alternated sessions with a wonderful dog named Benjie at a care center for homeless, emotionally disturbed people. Sunny and Benjie helped one of the residents overcome her intense fear of animals.

Frequently, I'm asked if I like other animals. Indeed I do! In fact, I also treat dogs if they have emotional problems. I really think "my guys" would do well with a dog. Perhaps the right man will provide the right dog to our domestic circle. Also, horses are a great passion of mine. When I lived in Malibu I had a marvelous thoroughbred jumper named Capers. It was the late Capers who caringly taught me to ride. So it was only natural that I adored him and groomed and bathed him ever so lovingly. To expand my animal behavioral knowledge, I have become a volunteer zoo guide at the new and beautiful Central Park Zoo. Each Thursday morning I have the opportunity to observe wild animals whose behavior is so similar to that of my feline patients. It is a marvelous way to continue my education and extend my help to visitors of the zoo.

Although I do not have an associate as yet, there are those who have helped me with my practice in return for the information they could gain about cat behavior. Emily was the first such person. She read my Cat Fancy *column, wrote and asked if she could be my intern a few hours weekly as part of her prep-school program. This turned out to be mutually rewarding. Emily is now at Cornell Vet School, and there may be a day we'll share a vet-therapist relationship. I now have a young budding actress who does part-time work for me as a coordinator. She doesn't plan to pursue a career with cats but enjoys and appreciates feline contact and information. Morgan would be a fine cat therapist if she ever decided to change careers.*

For me to give the best of myself to my patients and care-givers, it is essential for me to be emotionally, physically, and spiritually healthy. I

12

take aerobic classes at The New York Health and Racquet Club, run races with the New York Road Runners Club, and Gulf Coast Running Club in Biloxi, Mississippi and have a physical fitness trainer come to my apartment for work outs. Sunny frequently graces us with his presence. He enjoys the up-energy. I continue to take classes and attend meetings to extend my intellectual and spiritual knowledge. I find a perfect outlet to share my love of books is in my volunteer work at St. Vincent's Hospital, where I take the bookcart around to hospital patients.

I'm always adding new techniques to my therapy treatment for my patients. Audio therapy is a discovery of mine that greatly speeds up a cat's recovery and increases a cat's stress tolerance. My first instructional audio tape has now been released. It is called The Cat Caring Tape.

I have never met a cat I haven't liked. There couldn't be a better incentive than this for me to continue to love my work the way I do – a day at a time.

13

1.

WHAT IS MY CAT
TRYING TO TELL ME?

"Sam, please be quiet. I can't stop to pet you now. I've got to get these cookies into the oven," I cried. It was a trying morning and I had to get the cookies baked and all kinds of sundries finished before I left for The Practice. Sam was annoyed because I had jumped out of bed before he got all of his morning cuddling. He's fifteen years old and being Siamese tends to make him score high on the vocal chords—piercing, to be quite frank. Baggins, our other cat and Sam's adopted kitten, is eight years old. He was curled up in one of their baskets.

I knew Sam would not be enticed to join Baggins until I had picked him up and hugged him—so I did. But when I put him down, he started vocalizing all over again. This was my cue to stretch out on the sofa so he could climb up and stretch out on me. So I did and he did and soon Baggins joined him. It looked like I wasn't going to get my sundries done, but I'd made Sam and Baggins happy.

Sam's tactics had been a bit more dramatic in his youth. If he didn't get my attention by simply talking, he would give me a nip on the hand or ankle, whichever part of my body was most available. For a while I thought he was just ornery; but I soon discovered that if I petted and talked to him, he would relax and start purring. Other times Sam didn't want to be petted but just to sit in my lap and be admired. If I tried to pet him, his tail would swish back and forth, and if I persisted, he would give me a silencing nip. Yes, he wanted contact but it became clear to me

14

that he preferred to control the situation. Sam taught me that when his tail started swishing, this meant "hands off." He didn't discriminate and treated our friends and visitors the same way. To avoid any hard feelings we just told anyone whose lap Sam graced what his terms were.

Sam and I have been together fifteen years now. Sometimes he has communicated his needs to me by actually talking, other times by the way he moves his body, and, if necessary, by doing something bizarre to attract my attention to whatever it is he needs.

A cat is a very sensitive animal. How he feels is how he acts. It is, therefore, very important to know how your cat is feeling. Since a cat doesn't intellectualize his feelings as people do, his feelings surface much faster. Some cats, like Sam, are very vocal, and although you can't always figure out what they want, you are aware that they do want something. There are other cats who express their feelings primarily through body language, such as a wag of the tail or the ripple of a back. If you are able to decipher your cat's feelings by how he expresses them with his body, you will be in closer touch with what your cat is feeling.

Often your cat can clue you in on upcoming events through body language. For example, your cat's keen senses can alert you to approaching visitors (which usually happens when I'm in the bathtub or shower). If Sam comes sauntering into the bathroom with an annoyed look on his face, I know that someone is at the door. On the other hand, Baggins's reaction to such events is usually more hysterical than annoyed. Instead of sauntering into the bathroom, he employs the run-for-cover tactic; the sound of the doorbell causes him to seek cover under the bed or in the closet. Other times, you may notice that your cat will run to the door or stand with his ears cocked—it's because he hears someone in the hall. Often it's someone you expect, but he got the message before you. This may give you an extra moment to dab on some perfume or wipe the cat hairs off your clothes, and make any last-minute touches.

15

Baggins will run to the door if it's my husband, Paul, he hears; but for almost anyone else, he will cock his ears, peer intently toward the door, and then run for cover. Not Sam, he remains right where he is—unless it's Paul, and he wants to spend the energy to greet him at the door.

If you're under the hair dryer or plugged into earphones, and your cat jumps suddenly out of a sound sleep off the chair next to the phone with a disgruntled look, you can be sure the phone is ringing. He might even flick his tail or whiskers or ripple his back to indicate that he's annoyed and wants you to do something to stop the noise.

Not only does your cat use body language to express things he's feeling about himself or to convey messages to you, he uses it to clue you in on another cat's or animal's behavior. If, for instance, you find one of your cats intently sitting in front of a closed cabinet or closet and you can't find your other cat, open the cabinet or closet and your missing cat will appear. If the "missing" cat is sleeping, however, he'll probably remain right where he is and your other cat will join him or try to take over his spot.

One afternoon, I returned home from The Practice and Baggins, as usual, followed me to the kitchen. Suddenly, I heard a far-off cry and started toward the living room. I had taken only a few steps, when Baggins darted toward the apartment door and started to scream. I opened the door and Sam stepped inside. Without my knowledge, Sam had stepped out when I stepped in. On hearing Sam's cry of distress, Baggins had immediately run to his rescue.

Now and again a cat will help to save his companion's life. Parker Pyne, a client's cat, awakened her person one night by screaming and pawing away at her ear. There was no way he would let her sleep. When she noticed that her younger cat wasn't on the bed as usual, she called out to her, but got no response. The woman stumbled into the living room and noticed that the half screen was pushed aside from the window.

Her younger cat, Putney, was sitting out on the window ledge. Fortunately, this woman convinced the cat to come inside without incident; she might not have survived a ten-floor drop.

If suddenly you find one cat constantly picking on the other without obvious provocation, there's a possibility that the victimized one is reaching sexual maturity or is sick. Your healthy cat is annoyed and anxious because he can sense that there's something wrong with his companion. His way of protecting himself is to lash out at the source of his anxiety—your other cat.

Clarence was a mature, altered cat who lived with his people and companion cats. Although his relationship with the spayed female, Toffee, was never "ideal," his people became alarmed when Toffee started to victimize Clarence.

As I reviewed Clarence's case history, which included chronic cystitis, and observed his facial expression and breathing, I recommended that his chest be x-rayed. X-rays revealed that he had a minor cardiac problem. I explained to his people that Toffee had sensed Clarence's discomfort and victimized him because he made her anxious. Clarence started taking medication. As he felt better, Toffee became more relaxed and stopped her hostile behavior. Luckily, his people were able to take care of Clarence's problem before Toffee's behavior became habitual. If that had occurred, the reconciliation would have taken longer. By properly interpreting your cat's message, you may be able to discover your sick cat's problem, before it becomes serious.

Sometimes a cat can sense and react to a medical problem in his companion long before the problem manifests itself clinically. Butchkie and Ebony were mature, neutered cats that had a compatible relationship. Therefore, their person was totally confused when Ebony began to hiss at and reject Butchkie. I recommended that we examine Ebony to make sure she wasn't experiencing any medical problems. When Ebony checked out all right, I suggested that we examine Butchkie. He was slightly asthmatic, but otherwise OK. Butchkie started taking some medication and I advised their person to give both cats extra attention and support.

Several weeks later, Butchkie's appetite declined and he appeared uncomfortable. Diagnostic tests revealed that he had diabetes. Unfortunately, Butchkie's condition became critical and he had to be put down. Ebony had sensed Butchkie's problem long before it evidenced any clinical signs.

The more you become aware of what your cat is saying to you, the better your relationship will be. Sam and Baggins are forever making this plain to me.

2.

ANTICIPATION

Cats are creatures of habit; their anticipation of routine activities increases their security and happiness. One of the highpoints of Sam's day is bedtime; here's why. Paul usually makes it to bed before I do. As soon as Sam realizes that Paul is heading toward the bedroom, he perches himself on the bedside chest. No sooner does Paul climb into bed and stretch out his legs, than Sam immediately arranges himself on top of Paul's pillow. He proceeds to let out a short cry and nuzzle the spread with his head. If Paul tries to ignore him, he starts pawing away. This convinces Paul to lift up the spread so that Sam may crawl underneath. Sam doesn't remain there but very quickly emerges to settle down on Paul's legs. It's almost as if he carries out his ritual to firmly establish that he may sleep wherever he pleases; Paul's legs are his starting point. If Paul isn't too engrossed in his bedtime reading, Sam has very little trouble attracting Paul's attention to get what he wants—he's taught Paul to anticipate his actions.

Cats teach us to anticipate their actions; they also express anticipation. Because their anticipation changes from one situation to another, they express it in different ways.

There's "eager" anticipation, which occurs when a cat waits impatiently for something, but he's annoyed when it takes too long. At bedtime, Sam gives a classic example of this. If the phone should dare to ring while he's reclining on Paul's legs, he flicks his tail back and forth as hard as he can to convey that he wants the talking to stop and the light turned off so he can get some sleep.

Baggins's first love is food. On any trip to the kitchen within three hours of his next meal, he darts to his dish, ripples his body, scrunches up his face, and screams while he impatiently but eagerly anticipates his dinner.

Whereas Baggins needs no formal dining invitation, Sam often has to be called. Even then, it's not unlike him to start and then stop while he waits to be petted—another kind of anticipation. Sam feels more secure and comfortable if he's being touched while he eats.

Baggins is almost as concerned about his litterbox as he is about his meals. Heaven forbid the litterbox should contain the slightest debris when he is ready to use it (and we're around to change it). If so, he'll wait for one of us to enter the bathroom, he'll flick his tail and pace around the box or perch himself on the toilet seat and stare at the box until we carry out his wishes. Sometimes he'll even run back and forth to the bathroom trying to attract our attention. If we don't get his message or innocently leave the bathroom without cleaning the box, he'll get even by leaving a pile on the floor. However annoyed I may become, I have to remind myself that Baggins tried to get me to anticipate his need so it wasn't his fault.

Another one of Baggins's pleasures involves the bathtub. When I take a bath, he first props his front paws over the edge of the tub and stares intently at me as the tub fills. Shortly after, he paces back and forth across the bathroom tile. If I try to ignore him, he walks along the ledge of the bathtub. It's when he meows at me that I finally reach over and pull out the stopper. As the water drains out of the tub, I drape a bath towel around my body so Baggins knows his time is near. As the last drops of water leave the tub, Baggins jumps onto the towel and stretches himself out. From eager, impatient anticipation, he moves to intense joy at attaining what he wanted—to occupy my bath towel.

Gable was one of our resident cats at The Practice who was another "water freak." His anticipation concerned drinking—he preferred his water straight out of the tap. To get our attention, he would jump up next to the sink and gaze intently at the faucet until we turned it on.

Another kind of anticipation is "dread" anticipation, which is when your cat knows what is going to happen next and doesn't like it. Baggins clearly illustrates this state whenever he sees our suitcases come out of the closet. All of a sudden, there's a big lump under the bedspread because he knows this means he and Sam are going with us. He wants to *be* with us but he prefers that we all stay home. To lure Baggins out from under the cover, we usually put his canvas traveling bag by the bed with Sam already inside, and when we lift the spread, Baggins will usually jump right into the bag. Sam and bags are his main security blankets.

If your cat's body ripples, and/or his tail flicks, and he runs for cover at the sight of the nail clipper, he is sending you another message of "dread" anticipation. Try to have someone else distract him by petting or giving him catnip while you trim. If this fails, you may have to resort to trimming his nails during his lazy or nap period.

It's not unusual for a long-haired cat to scoot to the top of his floor-to-ceiling scratching post when his person takes out his grooming combs.

An especially vivid sign of "dread" anticipation is the tip of a plumed tail sticking out from under the sofa when a cat is trying to hide from his person who's trying to wipe his soiled rear. Unlike Sam, who dashes to his bedroom basket for his morning pills, some cats whose daily medication can't be disguised in their food have trouble adjusting to the ritual, so they, too, run in "dread anticipation."

Kriko is an adult cat who perches himself on the toilet seat to urinate and uses the bathtub drain for his other business. When it's time for Kriko's daily medication, he first camps out on the

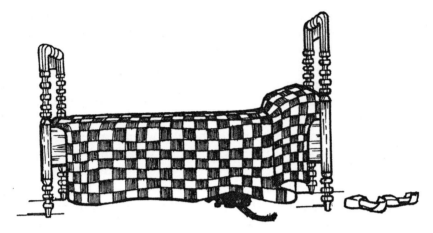

toilet seat for a while; if he finds this action doesn't distract his person, he runs to the bathtub. Although he gets his medication in the end, Kriko has found that as long as he seems to be attending to business, his person won't interrupt.

"Ambivalent" anticipation occurs when your cat both wants and doesn't want something. When we have visitors at home, Baggins will sometimes sit in the doorway to the living room washing and occasionally peering at us. He wants to join Sam, who is usually the center of attention; but he's not too sure about the visitors. Any sudden movement or loud noise will cause his body to ripple and he'll retreat to the bedroom until things have calmed down.

My friend Phyllis's cat, Barnaby, goes into a state of ambivalence when mealtime arrives. While Phyllis prepares the food Barnaby jumps up on the counter and stays nearby. Then he tries to show he couldn't care less by feverishly batting around the nearest unrelated object. However, by the time his food is in his dish, he's right there chomping away. Oh boy, does he want the food; but somehow, he's afraid if he acts too interested perhaps it will disappear. This behavior is characteristic of a cat who has had an insecure kittenhood.

Barnaby came from a pet shop and was the odd-looking kitten

of his litter. Phyllis noticed that he didn't interact with the rest of his litter at the pet shop. The other four kittens were cream Persians from a long line of cream Persians. Barnaby was a brown tabby. Since he was unlike all the rest of his mother's kittens, he didn't receive much of her attention. He probably remembers nursing as a traumatic experience. Chances are, he never got the nipple he really wanted when he actually wanted it if he showed his interest. Although this may be only an assumption, in fact Barnaby was a very sick kitten, which indicates that his relationship with his mother and litter was not fulfilling.

Jennings was a former resident cat who had a difficult time accepting affection. Sometimes he would nuzzle up to be petted; then his tail would start flicking as if he were going to spray and he would prance off across the floor. Although he wanted physical contact, the charge of energy he received from being stroked overpowered him. When this happened, he transferred the energy to another part of his body to decrease the overpowering feeling. As Jennings became more relaxed and accustomed to human contact, he was able to enjoy being stroked and cuddled without ambivalence. His major breakthrough came when he moved in with a cat named Rose and gained his own cat and person to love.

Anticipation is a natural expression for cats. It's important for us to be able to decipher their different kinds of anticipation so we can understand their needs. Once we understand what it is they anticipate, we can either go along with their wishes or distract them with something else. Thus we can decrease their anxiety level which, if ignored, can trigger various problems and disorders.

3.

HAPPINESS

As I have mentioned, Sam starts his night by sleeping on Paul's legs. Sometime during the night, he travels over to my pillow and curls his body around so that his face is nuzzled against mine and his front paw rests on my neck. All I have to do is stroke his head and his body fills with purrs.

Baggins sleeps all around the bed and often stretches out next to me beneath Sam. If he wants Sam's spot, however, Baggins will move right in. Then Sam will either walk around him and press himself between me and Baggins so he can have the prime position, or he'll just move to the top of the pillow. Of course he'll hiss and flick his tail to let Baggins know he doesn't appreciate his antics. If Sam feels Baggins is really out of line, he'll push him out of bed. Although Sam can be very ornery with Baggins, most of the time he indulges him because Baggins is his adopted kitten.

Many nights I'll wake up and find them nestled together against me. The look of bliss on their faces often moves me to tears of love and joy. There are many human couples who don't experience such complete happiness. By morning, either one or both start their jarring cat walk around our heads to announce breakfast time. Since Paul is usually the first one up and out, he gets most of the action. If he can't be convinced by their cat walk, Baggins will poke at Paul's mouth with a paw that isn't always velvet. After Paul has served them breakfast, Baggins will usually retire to his living room basket among the plants. There

24

he will stretch out on his back, with his tummy and legs a perfect bull's-eye for affection. Breakfast followed by a sunny basket makes Baggins very happy.

After Sam eats breakfast, he makes his way back to the bedroom, jumps on the bed, and lets out a cry to announce his return. I usually sleep facing the window; if I'm facing away, he'll circle back and forth around my head until I turn over. When I've assumed my usual position, he'll poke at my pillow until I reach out and pull him against me. Finally, he settles down next to sleepy me so I can stroke and kiss him. Soon Paul appears and Sam scoots down to his bedside basket for his morning pills. By the time Paul leaves, Sam is back in bed with me and insists that I stay until he gives me the signal to leave. This is when he starts his slow and lazy morning wash. It's his announcement to me that he won't object if I want to get up; he's had sufficient cuddling for the morning. Moments later, he'll decide it's time for him to get up.

To watch Sam luxuriously stretch his body up and then each leg gracefully out is like watching a superb ballet dancer. The only difference is that this morning limbering ritual is part of being a cat for which Sam did not have to spend years of study and practice. If I could start every morning like Sam, I wouldn't need yoga, jogging, chiropractors, and endless hot baths to release my aches and kinks.

Cats have many different ways of deriving happiness. It's an emotion that's unusually easy for them to communicate. One client tells me that her cat, Ms. Marple, is in complete ecstasy when she's sprawled out in their kitchen sink. It's not unusual for Ms. Marple to bring her the removable sink strainer as a token of affection. Ms. Marple probably enjoys the sink's coolness and feels relaxed and secure there. She is pure white, and it wouldn't surprise me if she has been admired for matching the sink so well. This positive association would reinforce her attachment to the sink. Cecil, her companion cat, prefers to recline on the sofa, so Ms. Marple has exclusive reign of the sink.

Butchie is a client's cat that adores curling up in any stray box or paper bag. His only problem occurs when he chooses a box or bag that's too small for his healthy-sized body. Like many other cats, Butchie feels safe, snug, and secure when he's curled up in the object of his choice.

Simba is another client's cat whose favorite pastime is jumping up to high, out-of-the-way places. To her, altitude is security and happiness. However, one day her person went to close the bathroom door. Simba let out a yowl as she jumped down from the top rim of the door to the floor. Fortunately, she suffered only a slight fracture in her leg. In spite of this incident, Simba still seeks the highest spots to hang out.

Mercury, a neighborhood cat, is happiest when he's riding on Brandy, his companion dog's back.

Harlequin was a former resident cat who would literally jump onto your shoulder or into your arms if he wanted contact. Once he was comfortably settled, he would purr and nuzzle away. He was too impatient to wait for an invitation. When he wanted to share his happiness with a person, there wasn't a moment to lose.

George Bernard Shaw is a former resident cat who walks on his front paws when he's happy or excited. His hind legs are congenitally deformed so he has become extremely deft and talented with his front legs. His rapport with his companion cat and person is not at all affected by his disability.

Piperoo is a long-haired cat who becomes ecstatic while he's being groomed. He runs to his combs and jiggles them to let his person know he's in the mood.

Buster Keaton is a young cat whose happiness involves the toilet. When he has to go, he perches himself on the toilet seat. No litterbox for Buster. When he's finished, he purrs and smiles. He probably feels special because his two companion cats use the litterbox and he's the only cat toilet user.

Much of O'Henry's happiness is linked with food. He now lives in Woodstock, but when he was a Practice resident, his nurses had to observe a special ritual or O'Henry would refuse to eat. He wouldn't eat near any other cats, so his nurses had to put O'Henry's bowl in a secluded area where he wouldn't be interrupted. We always knew when he was being fed because he would trail and trip the nurse who fed him, meowing all the way. As long as O'Henry felt the food was especially for him, he was happy and would eat away. Otherwise, he would turn his tail up at the food and walk on.

Sylvester and Keir are companion Siamese cats whose sources of happiness deserve mention. Most cats aren't fond of water, except for Keir! To him, a bath is a treat and his relaxed body and purrs prove it to his people. Sylvester delights in going through the motions of nursing Keir who, like himself, is male and neutered. Evidently, Sylvester didn't have enough contact with his mother and nursing Keir fulfills this need. Keir tolerates him for a while, but when he's had enough, he takes a walk.

Powder is another cat whose passion is extraordinary. She's an outdoor cat who adores the snow. When her people sprinkle bits of light snow over her, she becomes ecstatic. Sometimes she even rolls in powdered snow.

Sometimes you may accidentally find out what brings sublime happiness to your cats. The following situation is a perfect example. There is a couple who have a fair number of cats, but, luckily, they also have a large house and yard in which the cats can roam. Since some of the cats are leukemia positive, (that is, they demonstrate the presence of feline leukemia in their bloodstream, which is a fairly common malady among cats) they live separately from the other cats and have a special outdoor run. One day some grass fell into this run and the cats instantly devoured it. This made their people realize that although there was grass outside the run for the healthy cats to nibble, the enclosed cats had none. It wasn't possible to grow grass inside the run because of the steady traffic. But they solved the problem by providing the "grass-happy" cats with any stray grass they could find and supplementing it with fresh catnip.

Ned is a friend's cat with a great passion for heat. In the wintertime, Ned can invariably be found snoozing on his cushion in front of the radiator awaiting the steam. Loft dwellings are not especially noted for their heat and Ned is often disappointed. Although he sleeps with his people and companion cat, Buster, he's up like a shot at the first sound of steam.

There are other ways in which cats experience and communicate happiness that are not as easy to understand. Perhaps your cat has a laundry fetish! If he parks himself on top of your clean, warm laundry and kneads it up and down with his front paws, he does. This is a characteristic left over from kittenhood. When a kitten nurses, he kneads his mother in ecstasy. Some cats continue this motion throughout their lives whenever they are feeling good.

Is your cat a licker or sucker? One client tells us that his cat, Schwoogie, climbs up on him and purringly licks away at his clothes. This can be difficult if it's cashmere or silk that's being tasted. However, licking or sucking is another leftover nursing habit. Schwoogie was separated from his mother too early and he has an oral fixation. Licking makes him feel good.

Donald, Jr. is a friend's cat who is a nocturnal licker and nuzzler. Many nights he wakes her by licking and nuzzling at her hair. She manages to distract him with a few hugs and kisses. Another client's cat is a drooler. Sometimes this person wakes up in the middle of the night to feel his cat drooling in his armpit. Evidently, his cat associates hair with his mother's fur. His drooling occurs because he becomes overstimulated with happiness.

Bellyfeet is a "bumper." All you have to do is reach out to pet him and he bumps his head right into your hand. He's too impatient to wait for your hand to reach him, so instead he reaches out to you.

Often a cat prefers to call the shots and will dictate what makes him happy. I refer to this as "controlled" happiness. Our cat, Sam, is a born dictator. We are sometimes embarrassed to have to explain to visiting friends that although Sam wants to monopolize their lap, he might turn attack cat if they try to pet him. He enjoys the contact, but prefers to control the situation.

One Sunday afternoon we had some friends over for tea. Sam gracefully parked himself in Page's lap. This was her first introduction to Sam and she was quite flattered by his choice. Before we could warn her, she reached out to pet him, and he answered with a lash of the tail. We quickly acquainted Page with Sam's ground rules, and she immediately abided by them. In return, Sam allowed her a brief scratch of his head. Page commented that her cats, Louise and Trill, weren't nearly as demanding as Sam.

Another example of dictated control may be expressed while a cat eats. Lightning is a client's cat who rushes to the food bowl, starts to eat, and then stops. Although she enjoys the food, she won't continue eating unless her person pets her. When she's had enough petting, she ignores her person and concentrates only on her food. Lightning was used to contact when she nursed and sometimes needs the reinforcement of touch to help her enjoy her food. However, she'll make it obvious when she's had enough contact.

A cat devotes most of his life gratifying his basic needs and thereby making himself happy. You may have noticed that a cat's first commitment is to himself. Therefore, he is mainly concerned with pleasing himself. If this pleasure should simultaneously please you, you might call it coincidence or even a gift. A cat has innately solved one of the most important mysteries of life by using all his energy to make himself happy. Since a cat devotes his whole being to whatever it is he desires, his returns are multiplied. In addition, a cat is gifted with an exquisite ability to concentrate.

Generally a cat is self-motivated and therefore, can be very unpredictable or even downright contrary if you try to inspire or "force" his happiness—even if it's something that usually fascinates him. Baggins, our younger cat, loves to take jaunts in the hall, where he can observe the traffic to and from the elevator. He especially enjoys the compliments and greetings he receives from the neighbors. When he wants to go into the hall, Baggins will either try to climb the apartment door or sit in a total trance until the door is opened. If all else fails, he'll resort to hard-nosed tactics such as wailing mournfully until his wish is granted. Although he loves hall cruising, if I try to anticipate him and open the door for him to exit, he'll often ignore my efforts and wander off in the opposite direction.

Sam derives great pleasure from basking in the sun but if I try to place him in a sunny spot, he'll usually give me a grouchy look and amble away.

Although each situation is usually pleasure provoking, Sam and Baggins, like other cats, prefer to choose their own moments for various pleasures. Sometimes I find this annoying or frustrating; but then I remind myself that a cat does not respond to force even if I mean well. Sam and Baggins bring me so many moments of pleasure, sometimes when I least expect them but need them the most. If they occasionally accept my endeavors to please them, I can pride myself on interpreting their moods. Otherwise, I can accept the fact that cats are such experts at attaining happiness that Sam and Baggins will let me know what I should do to increase their happiness. As long as I continue to interpret their signals, I will become more adept at contributing to their happiness.

4.

SADNESS OR DISCOMFORT

"Oh no, Baggins, why'd you have to go and poo in the tub again?" I wanted to shake him but instead I just quickly cleaned it up. Well, at least he hadn't used the Hotel Carlyle's tub. This was a relief, because the hotel staff always gives our guys such a warm reception—especially Sam, who sometimes perches himself comfortably on the registration desk as we sign in. (We'd just returned home from there after spending the Thanksgiving holidays. Because of The Practice, we found it easier to spend our holidays in the city, where we could feel as if we were away yet be close by.) This was the fourth time in the past few weeks that Baggins had "decorated" the tub. The first time, I thought it was because his box was dirty; but the second time there was no such excuse. Paul checked a stool specimen but it showed no sign of parasites. The third time, there was still no apparent reason for Baggins to use the tub, and a second stool sample was again clear. Maybe this time he was upset about being away from home and his anxiety caused him to behave abnormally. Even so, it seemed best to check another stool specimen. Baggins is a very stubborn cat, but there had to be *something* he was trying to say. It just couldn't be plain stubbornness.

Well, there was something that Baggins was trying to say. His stool sample revealed that he had coccidia, an elusive parasite not always easy to detect. If it is not a severe case, coccidia, like many other parasitic disorders, can remain dormant until a cat is under some type of stress. In Baggins's case, the trauma of

33

being away from home triggered his problem. If he had continued to use his litterbox diligently, his problem would have remained untreated. But by behaving in such a bizarre manner, he attracted the attention he needed, his message was communicated, and his coccidia was treated.

Although this incident occurred several years ago, it is still vivid to me, because so many cats exhibit the same symptoms. Their persons, like myself initially, become annoyed and think their cats are being stubborn or spiteful. It isn't until I explain that their cats are uncomfortable and actually feel sad inside that these persons grasp the situation.

Sadness is not always an easy emotion to pick up on. Baggins's strange behavior certainly had me mystified because it seemed unprovoked and unreasonable. If indeed he didn't already feel sad inside from the sheer discomfort of coccidia, my intolerance of his behavior certainly increased his unhappiness. Once I realized he had a problem and his behavior was symptomatic, I could relate to how he felt. If it weren't for his unusual symptoms, he never could have communicated that he had an internal problem.

Sometimes a cat may refuse to defecate in his litterbox for reasons other than parasites or worms. He might be objecting to a dirty litterbox or might not like your choice of litter. Perhaps he doesn't want to share the box with an unspayed or unaltered sexually mature companion, because it makes him too nervous. In each of these cases, indiscriminate "littering" is meant to attract your attention so you'll remedy the situation.

When an altered cat urinates outside his box, this is always perplexing. Again, he could be objecting to a dirty box, unappealing litter, or an unneutered, sexually mature companion. Or—he's telling you that his bladder hurts.

It's not uncommon for a cat to suddenly chase his tail and to start munching on it. Often this is because his anal glands are full and are causing him to feel uncomfortable. This usually requires a trip to the vet, who will empty them out and possibly give an injection or dispense medication to ease the discomfort. Sometimes a cat's throat will become inflamed from licking away at his anal glands and he'll lose his appetite. In this case he needs treatment for both his glands and throat. Delilah is an adult cat that has a chronic anal gland problem. Her person can tell when Delilah's glands are full because she becomes constipated and strains in her box. Samson, Delilah's companion cat, also communicates the message by sniffing her rear. The secretion from a cat's anal glands is quite pungent and it's easy to realize why Samson is so attracted to it.

Once the problem is treated, your cat will perk up and he'll behave like his old self. If he doesn't respond to treatment, there's a possibility that another part of his body is the main source of his symptomatic behavior. (See Chapters 8 and 9, "Eating Patterns" and "Toilet Habits.")

Sometimes a cat will scratch around his face and ears until the fur has disappeared. He may have ear mites or inflammation from ear mites that needs to be treated. Another possibility could be an allergic reaction to fleas or food.

If you should notice your cat pawing at his mouth, he's trying to tell you it feels uncomfortable. Squeaky was a cat whose people noticed her pawing at her mouth after she finished eating. Since it happened a few times in succession, they decided to have Squeaky's mouth checked. It turned out that Squeaky had a loose tooth that actually fell out during the examination. Squeaky's paw was not adequate to perform her own dentistry, but it certainly gave her people the message.

Blossom was another cat who had a mouth problem. She actually had managed to lodge a needle in the roof of her mouth. When all of a sudden, she pawed and poked at her mouth, her person knew there had to be something wrong. Her veterinarian administered a short-acting anesthetic to painlessly and safely dislodge the needle. Blossom's person realized that needles would have to be stashed out of Blossom's bite.

One client's cat had a mouth problem that presented a double

whammy. She returned from a weekend away to find her cat, Tree Toad, pawing at her mouth. She managed to open Tree Toad's mouth, noticed empty spaces, dried up blood, and figured some teeth had fallen out. She disliked taking Tree Toad to the vet, since Tree Toad dreaded vets and became totally violent out of fear. But Tree Toad had to be examined because she couldn't eat and was beginning to drool.

It was necessary to anesthetize Tree Toad to examine her mouth. It turned out that she had lost a couple of teeth, but not where her person noticed the empty spaces. Tree Toad's teeth were cleaned and she started taking medication to prevent infection.

Gingivitis is an inflammation of the gums that can cause a cat to exhibit signs of discomfort. Freddy is a cat with chronic gingivitis. His person, Marcia, can tell when he's having problems by the way he eats. He chews his food loudly and appears to eat out of the side of his mouth. Once he starts taking medication, his gums feel better and he eats in a normal fashion.

When a cat is internally uncomfortable, his behavior becomes abnormal or bizarre so he can communicate this discomfort to his person. Generally, the problem surfaces during or is triggered by a stressful situation. Baggins's source of anxiety, for example, was a strange environment. The stress affected the most sensitive or vulnerable part of his body, which at that time was his digestive tract.

I refer to the most vulnerable part of a cat's body as his stress target. Often, as with Baggins, the sensitivity will disappear once the problem is treated. But in many instances, a cat's stress target will be threatened in various anxiety situations. If you can anticipate and minimize stress, there will be a lower incidence rate. Because emotional anxiety can trigger medical problems, the fewer anxiety-provoking situations, generally, the fewer medical problems. The following pointers will help you to make potentially tense situations less stressful.

1. Be sure to have someone come in and feed your cats twice a day if you go away for more than a day. It's essential that your cats have human contact. Since cats are such great creatures of habit, they dislike having their pleasurable habits interrupted. Even if at first they choose to ignore the person who visits them, at least they're receiving attention. Your cats are very likely to become depressed when you are away, and it's when their resistance is low that they are perfect targets for sickness. That's why

it's so important for you to provide them with special care during your absence.

2. If one of your cats is on any type of medication while you're away, increase the maintenance dosage a couple of days before you leave and a few days after you return. (Your vet can decide the dosage.) If your cat has a recurring problem for which he's received pills before, it may be advisable to medicate him while you are away. Again, consult your vet.

3. If you are traveling with your cats, a tranquilizer may be effective if they tend to become anxious.

4. If visitors come to stay with you, your cats may feel neglected if you're less available. An increase of any daily medication may be desirable at this time.

I cannot repeat too often that the happier and more comfortable a cat feels, the less prone he is to having problems. Although an emotional problem is sometimes the source of your cat's discomfort, it can trigger a medical problem. The medical problem must then be uncovered and treated. If at the same time, the source of anxiety can be determined and decreased or stopped, your cat will feel better and his behavior pattern will return to normal.

In each of the different cases I've just described, it was not always apparent that the cat was experiencing discomfort. It was even less apparent that the cat could be also feeling inwardly sad and miserable. There will be times when your cat's behavior will definitely indicate that he's feeling sad for reasons other than physical. I'll always remember how our cat, Sam, behaved several years ago when his adopted kitten Muggsy disappeared from our place in Malibu. Sam was so utterly broken up that he talked and cried nonstop. He couldn't bear to let us out of his sight because he couldn't be sure we would return. Since Sam was able to externalize his loneliness, and we were able to give him the extra love and support he so desperately needed, his longing for Muggsy didn't trigger a physical disorder. It was soon after

38

that when Baggins (whose entire name is Muggsy-Baggins) came into Sam's life and Sam has his *own* friend once more.

Christopher, my editor's cat, went on a sleeping jag after his companion passed on. It was his way of saying he was sad and lonely, and that he needed a new friend. Topper, a new adopted kitten, was Christopher's cure.

Because a cat has such an enormous amount of dignity, he won't always make it obvious that he's feeling uncomfortable. This especially applies to a cat who is critically ill. Pudding was an adult cat who had severe pancreatitis. As his illness progressed, his appetite dwindled and his activity decreased; but he still wanted contact with his person and his spirit was happy. It wasn't until very near the end that he occasionally uttered mournful cries to let his person know he couldn't cope with his discomfort. His person realized that Pudding's time was near because up until then he was too proud to complain. Pudding's discomfort was beyond his own tolerance but he was able to communicate the message to his person. His dignity was upheld to his last breath when we were able to let him go easily and painlessly with our assistance.

Sir Thomas was a young cat who was leukemia-virus-positive. He lived with his people, Phyllis and Conrad, and several other cats who were also carriers of leukemia virus. The healthy cats lived in a separate section of the house. In spite of his condition, Sir Thomas had boundless energy and spent most of his time in the outdoor run. On the coldest winter days Thomas could be found outside. Perhaps it was because he was an ex-street cat and still hung on to his rugged ways. Thomas was affectionate with his people on his own terms and he interacted with his companions fairly well. His closest relationship was with Gimpy, who idolized him. (Phyllis and Conrad · felt it was because Thomas had looked after Gimpy when he first arrived.)

Thomas received a daily injection of medication, which helped to control his condition; but he wouldn't sit still for the injection until he had been rewarded with a few brewer's yeast pills. One day, Thomas refused breakfast and showed no interest in his preinjection treat. That evening he jumped up on Conrad's knee and camped out on his lap. Thomas's medication was increased and his spirits brightened for a few days but then declined He continued, however, to seek his people out for attention as he had never done before. It was evident that his days were numbered. Sir Thomas passed on at home with his people by his side. They were grieved to lose him but he had managed to live a happy life for more than a year. When they buried Sir Thomas in their backyard, Gimpy appeared alongside them; he let out a low, chirping sound. This was his farewell to his friend Thomas.

A cat can be sad and critically ill but still carry an underlying air of survival. Roddy MacDowell was a former resident cat who was found in a cellar—abandoned, emaciated, and with a mutilated tail. Roddy was the thinnest and sorriest Siamese cat we'd ever seen. At first contact he was shy and wary. But after we'd cleaned him up and given him some medication, his eyes began to come alive. Medically speaking, his chances were slim, but something about Roddy's spirit told me he had a chance. We started him on a well-balanced diet with supplementary vitamins, treated him for his anemia and other disabilities, and waited to see his response. If Roddy made it, his tail could be fixed. But there was no way he could make it through surgery in his present debilitated condition.

As the days passed, Roddy's will to live took over. I know that the love and support he received from his nurses contributed largely to Roddy's survival. Roddy's surgery was successful and he was adopted shortly after.

It's not uncommon for a cat to avoid or reject another sick cat. Very often a mother cat will abandon or destroy a sick kitten to protect herself and her other kittens. There was a kitten trio that showed up at The Practice who had such serious upper respiratory infections, we didn't expect to save them. They were

Flopsy, Mopsy, and Cottontail. At first, they all clung together. A few days later, I noticed that Flopsy and Mopsy's spirits seemed brighter, but they avoided their brother Cottontail. That evening was a sad one—Cottontail didn't make it. Evidently the girls sensed how bad he was and kept their distance in self-preservation.

The two girls pulled through, but their coordination was affected by the virus. They walked like Mae West in reverse. Because they were left motherless so young, they needed constant attention and reinforcement from their nurses. There was no mama to nurse and snuggle them. They played and stayed together a lot, but I felt it best to have each move in with an older cat who could guide their whiskers. Mopsy joined Sylvester, a carefree young blade, and Flopsy went to live with Chin Chin, a bachelorette in need of a companion.

In some situations I've known a cat to comfort his companion to the very end. Parcheesi was a young, altered, outdoor male cat who lived with his person and companion cat. When their person went off to the West Coast, she left the cats in the care of a neighbor, but with free access to the street.

One day my friend Sondra, who lives in the same building, found Parcheesi mournfully crying beside the curb. She approached him and found his companion sprawled beside him. She'd been hit fatally by a car. Sondra took Parcheesi in her arms and they clung and cried together. After she had gained composure herself, she took Parcheesi up to her apartment but isolated him from her two cats. For a few days Parcheesi was withdrawn and sad, but slowly he responded to Sondra's comforting. Somehow her two cats sensed his need of her and they didn't try to invade his territory. Sondra's boyfriend was able to compensate by giving them extra attention and treats. Soon Parcheesi's spirits brightened. He had lost his companion but Sondra found him a new home with her brother in Columbus, Ohio. Parcheesi is now the pride of the household.

Very often a cat's grief for his deceased companion can bring to the surface a dormant medical problem. Stinky and Sheba were mature cats that were raised together from kittenhood and had a very tight relationship. Stinky had a long-term medical problem that finally became fatal. Near the end of Stinky's life, Sheba became sick. She passed on three months later, like a widow who doesn't wish to go on living without her husband.

Because it's hard to always know when your cat is feeling sad and uncomfortable, the better you can interpret your cat's behavior, the more in touch you'll be with his needs.

5.

RAGE

I couldn't bear to look at the clock radio; I knew it had to be some absurd hour. Although the air conditioner was going near full capacity (usually the air conditioner acts as my sedative) and Paul had pulled the quilt to the top of his head, I couldn't sleep. Rather than toss and turn, I decided to check out the refrigerator.

As I reached into the freezer, pulled out the vanilla Häagen-Dazs ice cream, and started to close the refrigerator door, there was a violent hiss and howl. It was Sam! He had followed me to the kitchen and, without knowing, I almost caught his tail in the door. Sam took it as a deliberate personal attack. I tried to apologize, but when I reached down to pet him, he stretched out to bite me. His ears were flat back, his pupils were dilated, his tail was fluffed, and his body was arched. Sam was furious and wanted none of my sweet talk. Although his tail wasn't really hurt, his dignity was injured.

I decided to forget Sam and concentrate on my ice cream. This turned out to be a very wise choice. Sam swallowed some ice cream in exchange for his fury. Sam and I very quickly finished off the ice cream. When he didn't object to my carrying him back to bed, I knew I was forgiven.

It's generally very easy to recognize when your cat is in a rage. His ears flatten, his pupils dilate, his back ripples, his tail jerks, and he emits a characteristic, unnerving yowl that may continue for some time. When your cat is angry, don't try to pick him up.

43

Instead, distract him with food or a favorite toy. When he feuds with his companion or any other cat, use a plant sprayer to break them up. If you try actively to interfere, you stand a strong chance of becoming the victim of displaced aggression.

The sources of your cat's rage may be varied and unusual. A friend told me that one day he was sitting on the bed removing his shoes when his cat started to sniff them. Suddenly, the cat started making guttural noises and his whole body puffed up. At first his owner thought the cat was having a fit. Then he realized that he had just visited some people whose cat and dog he had petted. Evidently, his shoes still carried their scents and his cat was enraged. He realized that as soon as his shoes disappeared, his cat would calm down. The cat was threatened by the scent of the shoes and his rage protected him against the threat.

Another time, I was visiting a neighbor when, without apparent provocation, her male cat attacked her female. They actually went around like a top until we were able to separate them by squirting them with the plant sprayer. My neighbor was flabbergasted! After all, Daisy just came in from the garden and Mac was fast asleep. Why should he wake up like a shot and pounce on poor Daisy?

I asked her if there were ever any other cats in the garden, and she replied that very often there were. I told her that Daisy probably brought back the scent of an alien cat or two which infuriated Mac. To him, Daisy smelled like another cat. She didn't smell like Daisy and he was disoriented by the strange smell; that's why he attacked her. Mac wasn't really after Daisy but the scent that she carried from the garden.

I advised my neighbor to rub Daisy off with a towel and then rub Mac's coat with the same towel. Once the smell was transferred to Mac, it would become familiar and he'd no longer be threatened by it.

Rage is an emotion that usually erupts quickly. Generally it is not a lingering feeling and disappears once the energy is let out.

It's not like anxiety, which is a state of apprehension, fear, and/or worry that can linger a long time, sometimes indefinitely.

If your cat goes into a sudden rage, remove the source if there is one you can identify, and stay out of his way. Then distract him with something that makes him feel good; his rage will quickly vanish.

6.

EXPRESSIONS OF ANXIETY

Sam was seven years old when Paul came into my life. At that time, Sam's cat companion was Oliver (who later passed on from leukemia). Both cats accepted Paul; it wasn't until I smuggled an orphan cat into the apartment that there was trouble!

Although I kept the visitor in a big, walk-in closet that had housed other orphan cats quite comfortably, this cat managed to get out. His timing was indeed dramatic! About three o'clock in the morning we were awakened by angry, guttural noises. Sam had the strange cat cornered in the living room. Paul tried to break them up by throwing his pillow in between the two. Unfortunately, Sam jumped from the pillow onto Paul's arm and sunk his teeth in. Paul cried out in pain and anger. Sam was confused. He didn't mean to attack Paul. At that moment, however, anything that moved was his enemy.

Sam felt insecure and endangered by the alien cat, and when he's anxious, he attacks the source of his anxiety. Although the alien cat was his target, Sam was so upset he couldn't discriminate. When Paul bodily interfered, Sam transferred his aggression to him.

Paul soaked his arm in ice and was able to prevent any serious aftereffects. Sam hurt Paul's feelings but Paul felt better when, later, Sam curled into his lap and purred. Sam felt a lot better when the orphan went off to his new home the next day.

Anxiety is defined as mental distress or uneasiness caused by apprehension of danger or misfortune; it is also used synonymously with fear or worry. Fleeting anxiety, which is quickly discharged, is *not* a threat to your cat. It's when the anxiety builds up and is not discharged that the anxiety turns to a pervasive fear and your cat's peace of mind and physical well-being may be threatened.

To avoid becoming a victim of your cat's displaced aggression, use water to distract and cool him off when he becomes aggressive . . . and keep your distance!

Unlike Sam, who fights when he becomes overly anxious, Baggins flees. One summer weekend we visited friends in the country. The last day of our visit Baggins disappeared. He and Sam were outside for a short jaunt when Max, one of our friends' cats, appeared. We thought that Max and his companion cat, Kali, were inside the house and were as surprised as Baggins when Max showed up. Luckily, we managed to lure Max back inside the house, and Sam didn't venture far. But Baggins took off! No one had spotted him making his getaway. At first, we weren't too concerned, but after repeatedly calling his name and searching the barn, we became very anxious. It wasn't until I decided to repeatedly call out Sam's name that Baggins appeared. Baggins hates to be left out—after all, Sam might get all the special treats. To make sure Baggins didn't disappear again, we deposited both cats in our room until it was time to leave.

Neither Sam's nor Baggins's reaction to an alien cat is easy to deal with and the best alternative for us is to anticipate similar anxiety-provoking situations and try to prevent them.

Sometimes the arrival of an alien cat may be totally unpredictable. Rosenante is a four-year-old cat that lives with her two-year-old companion, D.Q. Both cats are neutered. One night an alien cat entered their apartment through an open window and was there just long enough to terrify Rosenante and startle their person. The next morning Rosenante hissed and batted at D.Q. for no apparent reason. Their person, Peter, called me in a frenzy; he couldn't understand Rosenante's bizarre reaction to D.Q.

I explained to him that Rosenante was traumatized by the alien cat who was the source of her anxiety. Because she was so upset, she couldn't discriminate and transferred her hostility to D.Q. Although he wasn't the source of her anxiety, he became its object or victim. It wasn't until Rosenante could relieve her anxiety that she could relax and interact normally with D.Q. I recommended that Peter remain calm and comfort and reassure Rosenante. I also told him that a tranquilizer would help to relieve her anxiety and that it was probably necessary to keep her on it for only a couple of days.

In each of these situations, an alien cat was the source of anxiety, but each outcome was different. In Sam's situation, his anxiety caused him to accidentally transfer his hostility to Paul. Rosenante's target was D.Q. Baggins's reaction to anxiety—running for cover—was the least offensive.

There is, of course, a certain amount of everyday anxiety your cat experiences that is harmless and easily released. "Expectation" anxiety is an example. You hear your cat making a chutter-chutter noise and see him flex every body muscle as he prepares to catch that bloody old fly. Generally your cat succeeds, his anxiety is relieved, and gratification is his. It's when the fly outwits him that your cat's chutter-chutter gives voice to his temporary frustration. If this should happen, you might distract him with food or a favorite toy.

You may sometimes experience your cat's "overstimulation" reaction. You are stroking him and he appears to be enjoying it. All of a sudden, you feel his teeth sink into your hand. "What a fine thank you!" you scream at him. It probably occurs to you that he doesn't want to be petted any longer. However, your petting has aroused him so much that he couldn't handle the energy charge. At first he felt good, but the intensity was too great. He became anxious and finally aggressive. If this frequently happens with your cat, give him shorter doses of petting

until his acceptance tolerance increases. The following incident is a perfect example of an "overstimulation" reaction.

Balzac is a massive, black, one-eyed ex-street cat. He was rescued from being hanged but had already been caught in a muskrat trap where he lost a couple of toes. Balzac's "well-wisher" had been an artist who strove to annihilate Balzac for spraying on his sculpture.

It took a couple of weeks before Balzac's wounds began to heal and he was well enough to be altered. Because he was difficult to treat, we tried to tranquilize him, but to no avail. As the days passed, he became a bit more trusting but remained unpredictable. He would allow you to pet him and even show signs of relaxing; but just when you relaxed, he'd let you have it. Fortunately, he had a few teeth missing.

Balzac reacted this way because when he became too aroused he couldn't handle the energy. He nipped you because you were the source of his conflict. Because of his traumatic past, it was difficult for him to relax and his anxiety level was high. He could only deal with small doses of stimulation.

Balzac's cure came after he moved in with a black kitten named Kelly. By roughhousing and interacting in a cat-to-cat relationship, Balzac was able to work out his anxiety. His acceptance tolerance even increased to a point where he would curl into bed with his people each night and purr away.

"Unfulfillment" anxiety can often occur when an unspayed, sexually mature female and altered male live together. When the female goes into heat the male will usually start his mating act by biting her on the neck. From start to finish she's dissatisfied because he can't completely fulfill her and he's dissatisfied because of her weak response. Because her sexual energy level is so much higher than his, it's difficult for them to reach fulfillment together. If this situation repeats itself too often, chances are that the stress will trigger physical problems for your male, and your female is prone to becoming difficult to live with. Spaying her will allow all of you to live in harmony unless you are willing to cope with a litter of kittens each time she's in heat.

Although most of the time a cat washes to groom himself, a cat will often wash when he's anxious. Tiffany and Hobbit are adult cats who sometimes travel in the car with their family. As soon as they are placed inside the car, they begin to wash each other. The car makes them anxious and by washing each other, their energy is transferred to the motions of washing. Contact and warmth are provided by washing. This is a pleasant feeling because it's a positive association for a cat with a mother-kitten relationship which provides security.

You may be surprised to find your cat reacting poorly to your preparations for a holiday away. While you're calmly and casually trying to go about your preparations, you notice his appetite is off and his chronic eye problem has returned. Sure enough, your cat is reacting to "separation" anxiety.

A client couldn't understand why his cat, Carmen, was pouting and ignoring him. He mentioned that he planned to fly to Rome in six weeks for an extended visit but Carmen was to remain with a friend. I explained that Carmen was depressed because she felt something unusual was happening. True, she didn't know what it was but she could instinctively sense his excitement and it made her anxious. A cat is a creature of habit and is threatened by change.

Carmen's person, Kevin, insisted that Carmen couldn't be upset by his travel plans since he had hardly made any arrangements at all and his trip was still six weeks away. However, on second thought he realized that he did have extensive phone conversations, some very involved and excited, and that he was away from home for longer periods of time. I suggested that he try to spend more time with Carmen and provide her with special treats. Perhaps he could even arrange to take her along.

Several days later he called to announce that Carmen was joining him. He'd called the airlines and made a reservation for her to travel with him in the cabin. He eagerly added that once again she was the old Carmen.

Sometimes a surprise or change in routine can cause a cat to have an anxiety attack. Odie is a six-year-old altered male who lives with his people and companion cat, Freddy, who's neutered and the same age. Of the two, Freddy has always been the dominant figure while Odie tends to be nervous and shy.

One day, delivery men arrived with a new mattress, which terrified Odie. He immediately headed toward the bedroom, his usual, safety retreat. Unfortunately, the delivery men invaded Odie's favorite hideaway with the new mattress and he had to flee to another room. That evening he was tense and restless. When Freddy had a minor vomiting fit over his dinner, Odie's anxiety erupted and he took his aggression out on Freddy. His

people managed to break them up and calm Odie down, but later that night the cats chased and fought. Although Odie and Freddy were separated for a while and then put into the other's territory, there was no improvement. Each continued to hiss and growl at each other and Freddy had the upper hand.

I explained to their people that the delivery men had triggered Odie's feelings of insecurity when they intruded on his retreat. That evening when Freddy vomited, Odie grabbed the opportunity to take out his aggression on Freddy. I recommended that both cats be started on a tranquilizer to relieve their anxiety and that Freddy have a physical examination to make sure he didn't have any underlying medical problem that threatened Odie. Freddy's examination revealed a congenital heart murmur, but it wasn't causing any clinical problems. However, his people were now aware of his condition and would take him for periodic checkups to make sure he didn't develop any problems.

Freddy and Odie needed a large dosage of tranquilizers to calm them down, but were soon interacting without any major blowups. A few weeks later, they were able to tolerate each other in bed at night and they started to play. During this readjustment period, I emphasized that Freddy and Odie would need much positive support to make them feel better; their people couldn't leave it all up to the tranquilizers. I also reminded them that they shouldn't try to taper the tranquilizer dosage too quickly because it would take a while for their stress tolerance to increase and stabilize. Although Freddy and Odie had made steady progress, their condition was still questionable and any setback would only delay the healing time.

When a cat suffers from anxiety that can't be allayed by positive support from his person(s) and companion cat(s), auxiliary support may be needed in the form of a tranquilizer. (If the emotional anxiety has triggered a physical problem, they should be treated simultaneously.)

Cats do not become addicted to tranquilizers. As the cat's stress tolerance increases to the point that he can interact on a reasonably sustained day-to-day basis, the tranquilizer dosage may be decreased. However, if a setback occurs, the tranquilizer should be increased until the cat can cope comfortably, and then slowly decreased back to the maintenance dosage.

Once the cat's personality becomes well integrated so that he can interact and function without incident, the tranquilizer can be stopped. The time element involved depends on the cat's amount of anxiety, his person's support, and his individual healing ability. Generally, you can tell when your cat's stress tolerance has increased so that he no longer needs a tranquilizer: it's when he's down to an incredibly small dosage and he's constantly in a stupor.

Tranquilizers do not hurt a cat in any way when they are prescribed carefully by a veterinarian and given sensibly. The amount of medication needed differs with each cat and with each individual stress tolerance. When a cat is suffering from continued anxiety, he is hurting inside. If the hurt or discomfort is not allayed, the stress often precipitates physical problems. (Stress target areas vary with each cat—the skin, bladder, heart, etc.) The tranquilizer relieves the hurting inside. If a tranquilizer is used effectively to relieve anxiety, the prognosis is encouraging and optimistic.

A cat's initial reactions to tranquilizers vary—his coordination might become unsteady within twenty minutes to an hour after the tranquilizer is given. He may become disoriented and start talking. Since the tranquilizer makes him feel differently, he might try to resist the feeling by running around. Comforting and gentle talking will calm him down. Don't laugh at him! Tranquilizers are generally also appetite stimulants, so give your cat extra food (within reason) if he indicates he wants it. Sometimes your cat's dosage may have to be increased if he cries a great deal. Continuous crying usually indicates that he is still overanxious. You'll find that after your cat's system adapts to the tranquilizer, the above reactions are usually minimized.

Finally, at times when your cat is subjected to extra stress, such as if you go away or someone stays with you, when there are loud noises, etc., he'll usually need a higher dosage than his usual maintenance, to relieve his anxiety and to keep him from having a setback.

Positive support and a tranquilizer finally patched up Freddy and Odie's relationship; but in some relationships, that would not be enough. Brendan was a mature, altered male and his companion cat, Benjamin, was three years old and also altered. Benjamin had bounced around to a few different homes before he moved in with Brendan. He'd lived with a hostile and aggressive female cat in his last home. His kittenhood history was unknown, since he had been found on the street. Brendan had also lived with other cats before. Benjamin and Brendan's relationship got started well. They were together for two months before their problems started. Their person, Margie, went away for a week and the neighbors took care of the cats. When she returned, Brendan and Benjamin were hostile to each other. Fortunately, their anxiety was relieved by a tranquilizer and they resumed their friendship. However, a month later, their person went away for a weekend and she returned to two feuding cats.

Given Benjamin's history, his self-esteem was evidently very shaky and Brendan's heart condition made him very sensitive to stress. I explained to Margie that her absence upset their security, triggered their anxiety, and caused them to take out their aggression on each other.

Benjamin's experience with his former female companion cat only added to his insecurity. Since this female cat's people took care of Benjy and Brendan while Margie was away, quite possibly they carried her smell to Benjy—which added to his threatened state. I recommended that both cats be started on tranquilizers again, and emphasized that they would need constant reassurance. When they appeared mellow, Margie could put them together to see how they interacted.

Unfortunately, after several attempts, both cats were still hostile. With Brendan's heart condition and Benjy's low self-esteem, the best solution was to find Benjy a new home in which he'd be the only cat or he'd be with a kitten. Margie didn't want to part with Benjy but she knew it was best for all of them. So she did.

It is common for cats who are unaccustomed to children to have anxiety reactions to them. Dennis and Knicker-Mat are both two years old and live with their person, Wendy. Occasionally, a ten-year-old neighbor drops by to visit. He's a very outgoing and high-energy child; although he tries to move slowly and quietly, both cats retreat under the bed when he arrives. The best way for this boy to get acquainted with the cats would be for him to visit more frequently and feed them. In that way, they would become used to his activity and would associate his presence with food. This positive association would motivate them to hang around when he visits instead of anxiously retreating.

Albert is a six-year-old cat whose behavior was definitely affected by the arrival of a newborn baby. His immediate reaction was to urinate upon his people's bed. Because Albert had given this performance before when he was upset or anxious, his people had no doubts that he was reacting to the baby. However, there was another factor of which they weren't aware. When

Albert kept up his unusual behavior for several nights, they decided to investigate and took him to The Practice.

Upon x-raying Albert's chest, it was discovered that he had bronchial asthma. Because the baby's high-energy level was hard for him to deal with, he became anxious; when this happened, it became difficult for him to breathe comfortably. The discomfort in his lungs triggered the reoccurrence of the spasms in his bladder. Albert was started on medication for his asthma and bladder to control his medical problems. I explained to his people that his anxiety reaction to the baby triggered his medical problems, which caused him to behave adversely. Since Albert would have to adapt to the baby, he would need the medication long enough so that his stress tolerance would increase to a point where the baby's energy level wouldn't affect his stability. I suggested also that they make a special effort to give Albert more attention. His relationship with their dog and other cats would serve as positive reinforcement.

When people can anticipate and be sensitive to their cat's needs, before and after their baby's arrival, their cat's anxiety level will suffer minimal damage.

Christina was a fifteen-year-old cat and her companion cat, Sadie, was seven. They were accustomed to a nonchild environment. When their people decided to have a child, they realized that Christina and Sadie would have to make a major adjustment. To prepare them for the baby's arrival, I suggested they use a small amount of baby powder and lotion on their skin, so the cats would get accustomed to the smell. In addition, they should let the cats become familiar with the baby's furniture, etc.

The day baby Jessica was brought home from the hospital, her happy parents introduced each cat to her separately. Both cats were terrified and ran under the sofa. Because the cats slept with these people at night, they put louvered doors on Jessica's room and installed an intercom. This enabled them to be in contact with Jessica. Rather than cultivating hysteria by overreacting whenever the cats went near the baby, they supervised and remained calm.

As the days passed, the cats began sleeping under Jessica's crib. However, as the baby started receiving more and more attention, Sadie refused to eat. She became so upset that she even tried to imitate Jessica; she jumped in the carriage or sat on the baby seat whenever it was vacant. Her people realized that Sadie thought she would get more attention that way and that's why she was identifying with Jessica. Since they were aware that Sadie felt hurt and neglected, they made an extra effort to devote attention to her. Sadie responded rapidly and snapped out of her depression. Christina, who is not as highly sensitive as Sadie, was not so threatened by Jessica.

Jessica is now ten months old and the cats have formed a special relationship with her. Although they run for cover if she plays too roughly with them, when Jessica cries, the cats also cry in sympathy and anxiety. When Jessica is bathed they again become anxious and cry. They seem to sympathize with her feelings and even feel protective toward her. Because Christina and Sadie's people considered their feelings and worked out the problems rationally, both cats and baby now interact on a comfortable level.

Sometimes a person's anxiety can affect their cat's peace of mind. I have definitely found that Sam and Baggins are very sensitive to my anxious moods. If I return home with a lot on my mind, no time to spare, and less time to spend with them, they waste little time in letting me know that they are upset. As I quickly and anxiously run around taking care of the plants and the rest of my chores so I can get to my writing, Sam and Baggins also run around quickly and even more anxiously, that is, they run races between the living room and bedroom. If that doesn't "grab" me, Baggins throws himself at the apartment door to be let out and Sam wails pathetically to the tune of "You're Breaking My Heart." At that point they've made their case and I stop what I'm doing and adjourn to the sofa.

At first they pretend not to notice me and even run a few relay races over my body. But eventually Sam makes his way over to the sofa, taking the longest route possible and stopping dead in his tracks if he thinks I'm waiting for him. Finally, he makes it over and stretches out on my body; Baggins follows suit and settles in after he has kneaded out a choice spot on my chest or stomach.

There have been times, however, when because of top-drawer priorities, I've had to ignore their pleas for my attention. When this occurs, Sam will display his anxiety either by refusing a meal, which his slender frame cannot afford to miss, or by beating up Baggins. Unlike Sam, Baggins's desire for food will spiral with anxiety and he may even have a strained bowel movement. Fortunately, these incidents have been few and only often enough to let me anticipate what will happen if their anxiety goes unheeded.

A friend mentioned how his cats, who are usually low-keyed, reacted to an anxiety-filled incident in his home. One afternoon both his babies were crying nonstop, and his wife was in the midst of typing a thesis. He was trying, with miniscule success, to comfort the babies, and there was a construction crew working full blast outside the house. As the tension mounted, his two cats, Renfield and Bungee, began hissing at each other and then started to box. Fortunately, he was able to distract them with a snack and move them to a quiet part of the house until things calmed down.

Brutus is a high-strung cat who is overtly affected when his person, Martin, is anxious. One day, Martin was feverishly preparing a television production. He had little or no time to devote to Brutus and all of his movements were very abrupt. Brutus's first reaction was to shred the toilet paper into the shape of a pyramid. When this failed to get Martin's attention, he transferred his displeasure to Martin's girlfriend. If she passed him by too quickly, he took a fast swat at her. (Because he was anxious, any sudden display of energy upset Brutus.) He preferred to transfer his aggression to Martin's girlfriend rather than to his companion cats, Bridget and Martin. Although Martin was the source of Brutus's anxiety, Martin is also Brutus's number one person; it was easier for Brutus to pick on Martin's girl-friend.

Sometimes a cat remembers and relives a traumatic experience when he feels threatened. If he then attacks to protect himself, the anxiety level of both cat and people can accelerate rapidly. Tinkerbelle was a nine-month-old Siamese cat who was found abandoned by a building superintendent. Anitra brought her in to be checked over and spayed so that eventually she could find her a home. She mentioned that Tinkerbelle had bitten her and she was afraid it might happen again.

It was apparent that Tinkerbelle was very high-strung. We hoped that after surgery she would relax and feel secure. Tin-kerbelle's surgery went well and she was started on a tranquilizer to ease her anxiety. During her stay at the hospital she was very "head-shy" and almost cowered if you tried to pet her. Other times, she would hiss and strike out. I told Anitra to keep Tin-kerbelle separated from her other cats and try to provide her with a quiet environment. Evidently, it would take a while before Tinkerbelle's stress tolerance would increase to a point where she wouldn't feel threatened and unsafe. Perhaps her former person had mistreated her for crying and/or going into heat. Although I could only speculate as to what chain of events led up to her abandonment, Tinkerbelle was traumatized by it.

It took a while to regulate the right maintenance dosage for Tinkerbelle's tranquilizer. The objective was to get her to the point where she wasn't easily stressed. By relieving her anxiety, she would be able to cope on a day-to-day level. Anitra remarked that she constantly cried to be held and petted. I explained that she should try to give Tinkerbelle as much attention as possible. She could sit and read with Tinkerbelle but not perform any vigorous activity around her that might make her become anx-ious. Also, if she herself became anxious, Tinkerbelle would pick up the nervous energy, become threatened, and strike out to protect herself.

Anitra called one day in a panic. She had taken a friend to visit Tinkerbelle and Tinkerbelle's reaction was horrendous. Shortly after her friend entered the room, Tinkerbelle shrieked and would have attacked her friend if they hadn't made it out the door quickly. I asked if this friend was a high-energy person and found out she was. I explained that it was vital to Tinkerbelle's recovery not to subject her to "hyper" or tense people. Unless she was certain that Tinkerbelle would react calmly to her friends, an introduction was risky—for the friend or even for Anitra. Tinkerbelle would improve but time and patience would be the great determining factors.

For a while it was better for Tinkerbelle to be sedated to a point where she wasn't easily threatened. A tranquilizer was supportive, but her greatest strengths were reassurance and love. When her stress tolerance had increased until she wasn't vulnerable to everyday anxiety, her tranquilizer could be slowly tapered and finally stopped. In time, I told Anitra, Tinkerbelle should be able to interact well with an adopted kitten. In fact, I mentioned that if she knew anyone who had a kitten in need of a companion, this might be Tinkerbelle's answer. Of course, I explained that Tinkerbelle's new person would have to be able to understand Tinkerbelle's nervous disposition and be able to provide the necessary support. Anitra asked if this ever happened with other cats. She was beginning to feel Tinkerbelle would always have a problem. I told Anitra I had treated other cases similar to Tinkerbelle's.

My most dramatic and unforgettable case was Cary Grant, also known as the "Siamese warrior." I named him Cary Grant because I thought the name might calm his ways. Cary was brought to us, a tomcat who'd been hanging out in an apartment basement. Although the client had brought him to have his eye treated, it seemed best to alter him. This would allow his eye to heal better and, therefore, his chances for adoption would be greater. We did, in fact, know of someone who wanted a Siamese cat.

Cary made it quickly apparent, however, that he wasn't ready to move in with anyone. Cary had a problem. He was a biter and when he bit, he didn't fool around! When Cary felt threatened, he would rise to action, even out of a sound sleep. To begin, he would hypnotize you with his penetrating eyes and his body muscles would violently contract. Then, he'd give a menacing yowl, his back would ripple, and like a streak he would spring and sink his teeth into whatever part of you he could reach. Generally, he would attack your legs because they moved.

Cary's targets were primarily anxious people, usually men, because of their high energy levels. I realized that Cary was suffering from an anxiety reaction. He had experienced some traumatic incident from which he had never recovered. Therefore, whenever Cary was exposed to anxiety he would attack the source. Only then would he be able to protect himself against the pain and discomfort that anxiety triggered. Unlike a person who, in general, will depend initially on his diplomatic skills to protect himself, a cat depends on his physical strength. Nature is much more elementary than man when it comes to self-preservation.

Since Cary was so vulnerable to anxiety, I thought it was necessary to keep him in a separate room and to supervise his visits. I provided him with almost constant nursing care by nurses whose energy level did not threaten him. Most of Cary's day would be spent in a comfortable lap. His exquisite ability to let his body relax completely and "breathe in" love and attention was as powerful as his ability to attack when he felt threatened. Thus, Cary was an incredible barometer of tension. His ability to emphathize was great when it came to being aware of just how relaxed was the possessor of any particular lap. I remember one time he sat in my lap and started to swish his tail and glare at me. At first I was confused and even apprehensive; then I realized I was tense. It wasn't until I relaxed both my mind and body that Cary relaxed and curled up in my lap.

Although positive support was Cary's primary medication, Valium was his auxiliary support. (Valium is an extremely effective skeletal muscle relaxant.) He needed all the help he could get to relieve his anxiety. Although Cary started improving, he also had setbacks. His most violent one was when he attacked Paul, his veterinarian! Following this attack, Cary would rage at even the sound of Paul's voice. Paul could no longer enter Cary's room, which at that time was also our office. Fortunately, Cary's main problem by this time was no longer medical.

Clark Gable, a three-month-old black kitten, became Cary's top therapist. Gable could do Cary no wrong—Cary did not even mind when Gable sat on him. This usually happened when Gable wanted Cary's basket. Soon after Gable's arrival, Paul built a special room for them in the back of the hospital. Shortly after, they were introduced by accident to Browning, a very timid gray and white kitten who was Gable's age. Browning adored Cary; although Cary never hurt Browning, he only had eyes for Gable. Gable played with Browning but Cary was his "man."

As Cary's relationship with Gable grew stronger, his interaction with people improved. He was not so dependent on people's attention and the self-possessed attitude that he outwardly displayed became an inner reality. As his stress tolerance increased, his Valium dosage decreased. His body trembled with anxiety less often; his setbacks were fewer and milder. After sixteen months, Cary no longer needed Valium and he and Gable became the hospital residents. (Browning had already been adopted.) What a thrill it was to hear people remark on Cary's mellowness and the "not a care in the world" feeling he radiated. Cary became so well integrated that he and Gable starred in a children's play I wrote called *Kitty in the City*. With a name like his the stage was a logical stop-off.

A few months after their "coming out," Cary and Gable were

adopted by Maria, one of their nurses. She was The Cat Practice's first nurse and had recently moved away from home into her own apartment. It was a brand new start for the three of them. In the three years since then, Maria has married. Now Cary and Gable live with two other cats and a dog. Although it is not unlike Cary to do a minor takeoff on one of his infamous cries when he feels neglected, it's hard to believe he was once Cary, the wicked "Siamese warrior."

Cary's story instilled Anitra with faith and confidence in a positive prognosis for Tinkerbelle. I pointed out that she should let Tinkerbelle's body be the barometer of her own anxiety. Whenever Tinkerbelle's body became tense or her expression pained, Anitra should make sure she was relaxed herself and then try to comfort Tinkerbelle. She should check that she was breathing freely and not holding her breath. Otherwise, Tinkerbelle would sense her anxiety and discomfort. In addition, she should temporarily increase Tinkerbelle's tranquilizer dosage until the anxiety subsided. If she could be sensitive to Tinkerbelle's vulnerable moments, she could anticipate an anxiety reaction and prevent an incident.

Several weeks later Tinkerbelle moved into a home where she was the only cat and her tranquilizer was slowly tapered. Yes, it would take time for Tinkerbelle to heal, but eventually, with understanding care, her personality would become so well integrated that she would not have to overcompensate to protect herself. Each day would bring comforts instead of reinforcing threats.

In both Cary and Tinkerbelle's cases, traumatic experiences caused them to overreact to any kind of internal or vicarious anxiety. It is impossible to go through life without experiencing anxiety, but the well-integrated individual cat is less affected by anxiety's negative tolls.

Physical problems can often be precipitated by anxiety. Chula and Didi were neutered companion cats whose domestic situation was upset when their person's roommate brought in a stray cat. Although their apartment was large, Chula and Didi were not completely isolated from the visitor. At first they expressed their feelings by refusing to eat. Didi's anxiety precipitated a viral infection. Her person could not understand why Didi was sick and the stray cat appeared to be perfectly healthy. Perhaps he was sick before and still carrying the virus. Because Didi was upset and threatened by the new cat, she was a perfect target for the virus.

Sometimes when cats are anxious and unable to relieve their anxiety, their breathing becomes affected. Didi's upper respiratory tract is evidently the most vulnerable part of her body—her stress target.

Anxiety can frequently be triggered because of a medical procedure known as *declawing*. A person usually has his cat's claws removed because his cat scratches and destroys his rugs and other furnishings. If the person realized that this surgical procedure could probably leave his cat with physical or emotional problems, he might devise a different solution to the scratching problem, such as a good scratching post.

Physical problems connected with declawing can include an adverse reaction to the general anesthetic. A foot may become gangrenous and have to be amputated if the bandages are put on too tightly. Hemorrhaging may start when the bandages are removed; these are only the immediate physical complications.

A common long-term problem occurs when an entire nail bed is not removed and some of the remaining claws begin to regrow. The regrown claws are usually misshapen and useless. Sometimes the bone may shatter, which causes infection and continuous drainage from the toe. If this occurs, the cat must have another operation.

Postoperative emotional problems can be numerous. First of all, your cat is confused and disoriented by the bandages on his paws. The throbbing pain in his paws makes him feel miserable and depressed. When he tries to stand up, he falls over a few times before he adjusts to the bandages. After the bandages are removed, he discovers his paws are different. He can no longer stretch his claws in and out the way he could before. He washes away at his paws to rid them of the strange scents. The scents disappear but the paws still feel different when he washes them. Long-term emotional problems can seriously affect the declawed cat's personality. Without his claws as his natural line of defense, he can become insecure and distrustful. He may overcompensate for his feeling and become overaggressive when he is in a new or threatening situation. He's more apt to bite, since he can't scratch, and a bite wound may be more painful than a scratch. Many chronic physical ailments such as cystitis, skin disorders and asthma can be triggered by a declawed cat's emotional reaction to the surgery.

True, a declawed cat doesn't *always* experience these problems, but why subject your cat to such a traumatic ordeal? Most declawed patients I've encountered are tense and their stress tolerance is delicate. One particular declawed male cat named Hector suffered from chronic cystitis. He was a terror to treat! His personality was a prime example of the declawed syndrome. Hector's people realized how he was affected by having his front claws removed and decided to never even consider having their younger cat, Sylvia, declawed. Unfortunately, they had to leave both cats with relatives for an indefinite period of time. When they returned, they were informed that Sylvia had gone into heat and so the relatives had had her spayed and declawed at the same time. But the vet didn't remove her front claws only; he removed her back claws as well.

I had the opportunity to meet Sylvia when she was hospitalized. Some of her claws had regrown and they had to be removed. Unlike Hector the fierce, Sylvia was shy and unsure. Because she responded to contact, we were able to give her a lot of support. However, I kept thinking to myself that if she still had her claws, she wouldn't be in the hospital.

Some people argue that if it's all right to alter a cat, it's all right to declaw a cat. This isn't true! A cat does need his claws to cope on a day-to-day basis. He uses them for balance, defense, and grasp. Declawing a cat is unnatural and cruel.

There is a simple alternative to keep your cat from ruining your carpets and furnishings: a sturdy scratching post covered with a sisal material and lined with catnip. You can make one yourself, but be sure that the base is strong enough to support the post. If not, when your cat tries to use it, the post will topple over and he'll avoid it. Felix, a cat-product company, makes a fine post. They're located at 416 Smith Street, P.O. Box 9495, Seattle, Washington 98109.

If you praise and reward your cat whenever he uses his post and spray him with some water when he uses your furnishings, he'll become more and more attracted to his post. Be sure to keep it in an accessible spot. If your place is large, get a couple of them. (If your cat prefers wood, you can construct a wooden post.) Naturally, if your cat can go outdoors, he can do most of his scratching there. But whether he's an indoor or an outdoor cat, you'll probably have to trim his nails periodically.

When my first book, *Cats Prefer It This Way,* came out, I was invited to go on the Tom Snyder TV Show. I was all in favor until the producer mentioned that Tom Snyder planned to have his declawed cat appear. I explained to her that I thought a television appearance might be too stressful for a declawed cat and that it would make me feel very uncomfortable. She relayed my message to Tom Snyder; he suggested I provide the cat. I decided to bring Scribner, who was our current resident cat. I must say I was apprehensive about how I would be received after turning thumbs down on Tom's cat. But Tom was a perfect host. He mentioned he was a bit annoyed with my rejection but he respected my feelings. The show was a huge success for Scribner. He was adopted the next day by a couple of viewers.

Cats are very territorial and are usually reluctant to share their comforts with other cats. Generally, they associate another cat's arrival with a feeling that there will be less of everything for them. The stray cat's arrival made Didi anxious about her needs; therefore, her vulnerability to stress was increased. Unless a cat is accustomed to sharing his environment with strange cats and/ or he's very tolerant, he'll communicate his feelings to you about new cats—usually in a very dramatic way.

Feire-Fez is a three-year-old altered male who had a violent reaction to a new cat in his house. He had a fine relationship with his companion cat, Balthazar; but when his people brought in House Plant, an abandoned, one-year-old altered male, Feire-Fez would not accept him. His people tried to keep House Plant separated for a while, and then switched territories so the cats could each get a good whiff of each other. Feire-Fez wasn't any better! Next, they started the three cats on Valium. Balthazar, who was the least aggressive, was most affected by the Valium. House Plant slowed down but Feire-Fez was still intolerable. He was so upset by House Plant that his anxiety triggered a urinary problem so severe that he became obstructed and had to be hospitalized for a week. Shortly after his arrival home, it became apparent that Feire-Fez would never accept House Plant. His people were lucky enough to be able to find House Plant a new home. They mentioned that when House Plant was outside the apartment door, Feire-Fez surprised them by going over to him and giving him a friendly sniff.

Feire-Fez was not willing to share his territory with House Plant, but could accept him on neutral territory. Because Feire-Fez was once an abandoned cat, he was threatened by having another abandoned cat on his territory. Possibly, Feire-Fez had been abandoned because of the arrival of a new cat; House Plant's arrival triggered Feire-Fez's past trauma, which caused him to react with violence.

Once House Plant departed, Feire-Fez settled down and his urinary problem became ancient history. Balthazar became even more affectionate than usual. Although he was indifferent to House Plant, Balthazar had, nevertheless, been affected by the surrounding anxiety. Now that all was calm, he could relax. His need for more affection was a delayed reaction to the anxiety that had prevailed.

When a cat becomes anxious and the anxiety is not released but rather intensified, his body becomes tense and it contracts. This makes him a perfect target for a physical problem. The most vulnerable part of his body will be affected. Didi's respiratory tract was her stress target. Feire-Fez's bladder was his stress target. Hopefully, in the future their people will be able to anticipate their anxiety and give them the proper support and medication, if necessary, to prevent an incident.

Sam and Baggins let me know by their actions when their anxiety level is uncomfortably high. It is then up to me to take steps to try to reduce or remove the source of anxiety so they may cope more easily. I try to be aware of their signals so I can prevent them from being affected by undue stress. The better you are able to interpret your cat's communication, the greater chances are that you will keep him from experiencing anxiety-provoking situations.

7.

CHOICE

Bowie was our first resident cat at The Practice. In fact, he was there from the day we moved into the office space. We found him Christmas day outside my parents' apartment building—huddling, shivering, and with a mutilated tail. Paul had to amputate the tail and it took Bowie a while to make the adjustment. Without his tail his balance was affected, so he had to compensate for the loss, which he did beautifully. At first, his motions were deliberately slow, but within two weeks, he was running around like a normal, energetic cat. He resembled a fuzzy, gray rabbit as the fur grew back on his hindquarters. Instead of a cotton tail, however, Bowie had hind fur that wagged.

Since we hated to leave Bowie alone at night, I catnapped Jennings, a wonderful hulk of a black cat, from a lady with a multiple-cat household. Jennings was two years old, very mellow, but very sensitive. He kept out of sight for a few days; but soon he and Bowie were washing each other. Bowie was a hustler and Jennings's poetic qualities were just what he needed.

Yes, in Jennings I had made the perfect choice for Bowie. So far we were batting a thousand. Bowie was content living at The Practice: he now had Jennings, and Bowie was everything that Jennings desired in a companion. Bowie possessed all the dash and glitter that Jennings lacked. Jennings possessed all the inner beauty that Bowie still had not developed.

All went well for Bowie and Jennings until The Practice started to grow and more and more cats started to appear. The stress of the competition became apparent in our two guys' behavior. Bowie reacted by spending his days at the publishing company on the first floor. The people were cat lovers and Bowie's charm (when it's on), was irresistible. All we had to do was open the door each morning and Bowie would shoot down the stairs. His departure was easy. It was returning at 5:00 P.M. that he dreaded. One of his nurses had to fetch him and coax him back with treats or he would let her have it—claws and teeth. As the weeks went by, "Bowie, you're impossible!" was a familiar cry. If he did not get out the door on time in the morning, he would tinkle on a client's coat to express his agitation. The clients did not appreciate his christening, which was quite understandable. Bowie's choice was no longer Jennings and The Practice. He was happy only on the first floor.

Jennings's response to the heavier client traffic was more subtle. First, blood appeared in his urine. Then, to worsen matters, he would urinate in the sink or jump up on the scale after a patient was weighed and leave a sample. We started him on medication and tried to make sure he received extra attention. Since Bowie was away most of the time, Jennings's daily routine was no more. Not only did he have to share his home with strange cats, but now his friend, Bowie, was only a part-time companion.

Jennings's urinary problem was only the start of his troubles. It was followed by a hunger strike that was almost his finish. Jennings's appetite had always been "four stars." When he started to just pick at his food, we knew he was really stressed. We tried to entice him with all kinds of treats but Jennings barely responded. He showed interest only in the hospital patients' food and would almost dive at their plates. He even prowled through the trash.

To make sure Jennings didn't have a severe organic problem, we took a series of blood tests and x-rays. The results did not indicate anything remarkable. Jennings's behavior was due to his depressed and frustrated state of mind. His disturbance was so severe that his will to live had been compromised. He was once a hulk and now he looked like a rail. Old clients would look right at Jennings and ask who was the new black cat.

Bowie was able to cope with the situation by choosing a non-threatening environment in which to hang out, where he didn't have to compete with an endless stream of cats that we fussed over and complimented. Bowie's tactics were hardly subtle. Jennings communicated his message slowly, subtly, and painfully. He internalized his anxiety and it tore away at him, whereas Bowie externalized his.

It was a hard decision because Jennings was so much a part of The Practice, but we knew we had to find another place for him. Two of our staff agreed to take him to their home with them for a while to see how he would react. It turned out to be an ideal situation. Jennings's appetite returned, his eyes regained their old glow, and he even took to playing like a kitten. Although this was only a temporary home, it was the beginning of a new life.

Two months later Jennings moved in with Rose, a coquettish Siamese kitten, who filled the void left by his old friend Bowie. His new person, Carol, quickly grew to adore Jennings as much as she did Rose.

Bowie's permanent transfer to the first floor was inevitable. We were sorry to lose our first resident cat, but there was no way we could make Bowie happy. Shortly after Bowie moved in, the people adopted Lorelei, a very mellow calico, to keep Bowie company. Frequently one or the other camped out on their front window, where we would stop and wave to them.

Given the nature of The Practice, it was impossible to provide Bowie and Jennings with the love and attention they needed. Some cats can adapt to living at a hospital where they constantly encounter other cats, but Bowie and Jennings wanted their own place. The Practice was only a stopover for them. They desired more, and luckily, we were able to fulfill their wish. Vanderbilt was another resident cat who became unhappy with The Practice; his source of discontent was Alfalfa, a young kitten who was up for adoption. Alfalfa was superenergetic and allowed Vanderbilt no peace.

One day a couple came in with their older kitten, Minnagold, who needed a companion. Since they wanted a kitten, I took them inside to see Alfalfa. However, Vanderbilt, who had been curled up on his cushion, jumped over to them and bumped away at their legs. (We had found him on the street and he still limped from an old leg injury.) Well, how could they resist an affectionate cat who limped all the way across the room to be near them? A few days later, Vanderbilt moved in with them and Minnagold, and everyone was happy.

It is not uncommon for cat companionships to come to an end because of environmental stress. Little John, a genuine street cat from the East Village, was adopted from us by a restaurant in a business area. When Little John wanted something, he was sweet as sugar. Otherwise he was tough as nails. His prime passions—food, catnip, and freshly ground coffee beans—made the downstairs kitchen his first hangout. But soon his need to be the center of attention drew him upstairs to the restaurant where he "camped out" in the middle of the floor in the midst of the traffic. Everyone had to stop and pet him, but if he wasn't in the mood, he'd respond with a nip. Although he was often the perfect host, some of the clientele objected to his presence.

We sent Lady Biltmore, an untamed gray tiger, to live with Little John, hoping she'd lure him downstairs again. Biltmore had lived in a parking lot where she received three square meals a day; but the other cats ignored and avoided her. Because she was untamed and not people-oriented, it was only by sedating her that we were able to get her, spay her, and finally send her to Little John.

Possibly, Little John was Lady Biltmore's first companion. She immediately fell in love with him. She ate only after he had finished eating and even washed his face. Although she hung out downstairs, Little John still preferred the restaurant. With his obvious chauvinistic nature, he probably didn't want his woman to share the spotlight with him. Unfortunately, the lunch clientele from City Hall strongly objected to Little John as their host. He had to go! Alas, he and Biltmore (after much sedation) returned to The Practice.

Little John was badly shaken by the stress of the sudden move. To him, it probably felt like he was at the orphanage again; what a letdown! He became so depressed he completely rejected Lady Biltmore and suffered an asthma attack. Somehow, someway, we had to find a new home for him fast.

California turned out to be the answer. Paul's brother and wife wanted another cat, so Little John flew out to northern California to live in a vineyard. He quickly won the hearts of the entire family. Along with the many other different kinds of animals, Little John had a harem of three female cats to treat him right, and an associate male cat to teach, who could fill in when Little John wanted time off. There was even Brownie, a dog, for him to bully as only he could. What a victorious move for Little John—host of the Ocean Club Restaurant becomes King of the Vineyard!

Little John had found his spot but his ex-lover, Lady Biltmore, was still untamed and unapproachable. Gradually, with the support of tranquilizers and patience, she began to accept some contact. But one morning she made the great escape! She managed to slip into the back of the hospital and out the only open window to the ground, three flights below. We searched the backyards and put up signs, but still no Lady Biltmore.

Several days later, the superintendent next door told us he had seen a gray tiger cat in one of the adjoining yards. One of our nurses lived in an apartment with a first rate view of that yard. I asked her to start leaving food out. Lo! Biltmore showed up for dinner. Over a period of weeks, by first leaving food on the window sill, then opening the window, and finally, putting

73

the food in the living room, this nurse induced Lady Biltmore
to come inside. One evening Biltmore's food was spiked with a
tranquilizer; she was lured to the bedroom and the living room
window was closed so she couldn't flee. We went over and Paul
was able to catch her by wrapping her in a towel. Soon she was
safely back at The Ocean Club Restaurant, and I found Ring
Lardner, a homeless black-and-white, altered male to accompany her. Ring was very timid and I assumed he would take
awhile to acclimate to his new surroundings and Biltmore.

Within two weeks Ring and Biltmore fell madly in love. They gave in to limiting their activity to the kitchen downstairs with only an occasional visit to the restaurant. It was evident that Ring was the perfect choice for Biltmore. The most remarkable outcome was that he tamed her. One evening we went to visit him, and Lady Biltmore strutted out. She actually chose to come over to be petted. Somehow Ring's acceptance of us had instilled her with trust and confidence so that she could accept us too.

Happiness prevailed with Ring and Biltmore until the health department ordered the cats "off limits." Once more Lady Biltmore returned to The Practice with Ring to accompany her, and once more there was a major rejection. Only this time it was Lady Biltmore who chose to be the rejector. As with Bowie and Jennings and Little John, the environmental stress of The Practice threatened Biltmore and she transferred her fear and hostility to Ring. He couldn't approach her without getting a full-blown attack. We separated them but not fast enough to prevent Ring from developing cystitis from his emotional upset.

After we pulled Ring through his cystitis, he went to live with another cat but this time in an apartment. No more restaurants for him! Lady Biltmore moved in with Bozo, a mellow, altered male. However, Bozo could not adjust to her unlimited energy. Her luscious green eyes weren't enough to melt him, so finally she moved to a home in the country.

In each of these situations, environmental stress was the source of the cats' companionship problems, and the dominant or most demonstrative cat transferred his anxiety onto his companion. Bowie and Little John expressed rejection without an outward display of hostility. But Lady Biltmore's stress tolerance was challenged too many times; so she took out her aggression on poor Ring. A cat's reaction to stress and anxiety depends upon his sensitivity, vulnerability, and previous experiences. These are the elements that influence *his* choice.

A move from a suburban to an urban environment is sometimes a difficult adaptation for a cat. Saba was a two-year-old spayed cat that moved from a suburban community to a New York apartment. In her previous home she was able to go outdoors, but a third-floor apartment drastically changed her lifestyle. Her person, Mary, adopted Keema, a young female cat, to keep Saba company. Saba and Keema developed a good relationship, but deep down Saba was still dissatisfied.

Summer arrived and one of Mary's roommates left a window open; Saba made her getaway. Although Mary posted signs all over the neighborhood and spent many hours searching, no Saba. She received several phone calls about various black cats on the loose, but when she checked them out, none were Saba.

Three weeks passed, and still no Saba. Then one evening someone called about an injured black cat that was seen in their courtyard. Mary went over only to find that it wasn't Saba but a black male cat. She called out to him and he limped over; so she decided to take him home to Keema who was very lonesome. If Saba showed up, she'd find another home for this male, whom she named Rudyard. He turned out to have a broken leg that had to be put in a cast. Then for a while he had to be kept in a playpen so he wouldn't overuse his leg. One afternoon Mary was pleasantly surprised to find Keema and her new friend, Rudyard, curled up together in the playpen.

Saba could not adapt to apartment living, and so she chose to leave home and make it on her own. Saba's departure brought Keema and Rudyard together and to them, living in the confines of an apartment was satisfactory.

There are some cats who live in city apartments but also get the opportunity to spend time outdoors. Hammett was a one-year-old altered male who lived with his person and three other cats. Because their apartment was on the first floor and faced a courtyard, Hammett and his companions had access to the outdoors. Their person realized the risks involved including traffic, anticat people, and aggressive tomcats; but he felt the enjoyment they derived from their outings compensated for the risks.

The cats usually went outdoors after breakfast and returned

home each evening for dinner. One evening, however, Hammett didn't return. Five days went by and during that time the other cats were kept inside. On the fifth evening, however, Fanny, who was Hammett's buddy, prowled from room to room and cried nonstop to go out. There was no other choice but to let her go. Their person realized Fanny was going to look for Hammett. Late that evening she returned alone, but when morning arrived Hammett appeared at the door. Fanny's efforts must have influenced his return. Alas, it was too late. Hammett had been severely injured and although his person rushed him to the vet, he couldn't be saved. Hammett had been hit by a car and had tried to nurse his wounds until he could make it home. His person realized that his other cats could end up the same way. Once more he'd have to decide if it was worth it for them to have the choice of going outdoors. Although many house cats go outdoors without encountering any major catastrophies, there's no way to predict the outcomes.

Sometimes cats who have the choice of going outdoors choose to move on to another home. Jaboo was a California cat who did exactly that. He used to live with his people, Judy and Steve, and companion cat, Hathaway. Jaboo spent most of his days outside chasing around the canyon. Before his people had him altered, he was quite the ladies' man and suffered numerous wounds fighting with other tomcats. His relationship with Hathaway was comfortable but not remarkable. Sometimes Jaboo would disappear for a couple of days; his people considered keeping him indoors but they knew he could never adapt. Jaboo was a roamer and they had to accept his way of living. They had found him roaming the canyon and they knew that's what he preferred.

There weren't any major problems until Judy and Steve found out they had to spend several months in New York City. Judy had to leave ahead of time because of business commitments. During that time Jaboo disappeared for several days. Steve posted signs of Jaboo's disappearance and received a

phone call from some people who had found him. They mentioned that Jaboo had visited them before and they didn't know he had a home. These people lived clear across the canyon. After Steve picked up Jaboo, he attached an identification tag to Jaboo's collar to prevent a similar incident.

As the time drew closer for Jaboo's people to make their big move to New York, they really worried about Jaboo. How would he ever adapt to the big city? Jaboo took matters into his own paws. Once again he disappeared for a few days and once again his people received a phone call from the folks he'd visited before. When they went over to fetch Jaboo, they mentioned their fears about the approaching trip.

Later that evening, Jaboo's friends called and asked if they could adopt Jaboo. At first Judy and Steve were hesitant but then they realized that Jaboo had made this choice for them. By the end of the week Jaboo had moved in with his chosen people. He never once returned to visit his former people. Instead, Judy and Steve paid him a visit before leaving for New York. Eventually, they knew they'd adopt a friend for Hathaway so she wouldn't be lonesome. As for Jaboo, he'd be fine. He'd made sure of that.

Patrick, a young outdoor cat, lived with his family and seven cat companions. He started making occasional visits to a neighbor and her two female cats next door. Soon he spent most of his time there and paid occasional visits home. Patrick evidently preferred the small family plan.

Gus was a cat whose choice of residence was influenced by the cuisine. One afternoon, our friend Dick called in distress. Lately a tomcat had been hanging out in the basement of his restaurant. The tomcat enjoyed the food they fed him and showed no intentions of moving on. This was fine with Dick until the day that Gus (as they had named him) left his mark all over one of the waiters' jackets! The smell was unbearable. Dick and his wife, Linda, didn't want to evict Gus, but Chelsea was a restaurant and not a place for a potent tomcat.

I recommended that they have Gus altered immediately and within several days he'd lose the urge to spray. Dick mentioned that he might have difficulty collecting Gus since he was a friendly but aloof cat. I suggested they put his food in a cat carrier and while he was dining, close the lid. Since they had all grown to like him, Dick hoped Gus wouldn't decide to leave after he had his surgery. It took a couple of attempts but they managed to collect Gus. His surgery went well and he made his choice to stay on as Chelsea's number one and only cat in residence.

Another situation comes to mind of when a cat's choice of residence was influenced by food. A client told us that one afternoon he stopped outside an antique shop to look at a chair. As he browsed, a cat appeared from underneath the chair. The client reached down to pet him and the cat reached up to inspect the client's package. There was fish inside. The client left without the chair, but the cat went home with him and the fish. Ambrose, as he named the cat, did some fine shopping that day.

There are also occasions when a cat will move on if his favorite person disappears. Cartier Bresson was a former resident cat who moved in with Dorothy, one of his nurses. Although he was friendly with her roommate, his eyes were mainly for Dorothy.

One summer vacation, Dorothy had to go home to her family and unlike other times, she couldn't take Cartier with her. She felt he would be safe with her roommate and their next-door neighbor. But when Dorothy returned two months later, she was told that Cartier had disappeared only a few days before her arrival. He'd made his getaway through an open window. Although Dorothy searched and scouted out the neighborhood, Cartier never returned. To him, home wasn't the same without Dorothy and he chose to move on.

Everyday living for Sam, Baggins, and every cat provides the usual routine choices to be made. In general they are communicated easily. However, the incidents just mentioned are not your cat's everyday experience. Because the cat who goes outdoors is exposed to many more variables than the indoor cat, his decision making is usually more complicated. But like Bowie and Jennings, cats who are exclusively indoor cats are often presented with a situation in which their choice has the utmost significance.

8.

EATING PATTERNS

We had just returned home with Sam and Baggins from Oyster Bay, Long Island. For the past two summers we'd been going out every week and staying overnight at a motel by the beach. The high point of our trip was to bicycle to the nearest Foodtown for several loaves of bread and picnic goodies. From there we bicycled to the duck pond, where we fed bread to the ducks. After they had eaten and quacked away, we settled down to our lunch—mostly a variety of tasty cookies. Whenever there was bread left over, which usually indicated there were many feeders before us, we bicycled to the beach and fed the sea gulls, who were always receptive. Although we couldn't feed ducks in the city, we often fed carrots to the horses at the police stables. Because eating is such a pleasurable experience, I derived a great deal of fun from providing the food.

As Baggins ran to the kitchen screaming for food, I reminded myself that although he'd eaten only a few hours ago, maybe the car ride made him hungry.

As I have mentioned, Baggins and food have a marvelous rapport. When Baggins announces he's ready to be fed, which is quite often, he lets out a persuasive cry. It's not a mew or a meow, but a long, piercing, repetitious "ow," which is very difficult to ignore. It is as if he's saying, "Ow my stomach hurts, ow my body hurts, ow I'm starving." There's no limit to what his pitiful "ow" suggests. Unless he knows that he is completely out of order, he continues to "ow" until the food is in his bowl.

Not so with Sam! I sometimes feel that Sam needs someone to ring a dinner bell and announce, "Dinner is being served." Whereas Baggins generally makes his entrance into the kitchen like a Mack truck, Sam plays the waiting game. He casually saunters into the kitchen, glides over to the bowl, gives a cursory glance at Baggins chomping away, and then exits. Shortly after, Baggins pulls himself away from his bowl and ambles out of the kitchen. Now Sam approaches his bowl and gracefully begins to eat. Once more Baggins appears and now they dine together.

Although Sam is twice as old as Baggins, Baggins is at least three times as big as Sam. Except for rare occasions, Sam always permits Baggins to eat first. This trait is characteristic in most relationships where an older cat and kitten come to live together. The older cat, like Sam, usually acts on an instinctive feeling, almost a maternal one, where he defers to "the little one." When we first adopted Baggins for Sam, it fascinated me to watch Sam step out of Baggins's way as he rushed to the food. Sam had done the same thing for Muggsy, his previous adopted kitten.

There may also be a selfish motive for this behavior. If, for any reason, the food is bad, the older cat's stomach is spared, and it is the younger cat who is affected. I write this with tongue-in-cheek because I really don't think Sam has an ulterior

motive for letting Baggins eat first. It could be, however, that Sam just doesn't enjoy Baggins's overexuberance and prefers to wait until Baggins is orally gratified before he partakes of his food. Baggins's style of eating can be classified as jitterbug or disco whereas Sam's style is more like ballet.

Besides being a delicate eater, Sam is also a moody eater. It's not unlike him to stop and walk out of the kitchen if we watch him or walk too close to him while he is eating. In the past couple of years, Sam's chronic mouth problems have increased and he only has a few token teeth. But his chewing handicap doesn't prevent him from chomping away on his dry food snacks.

Occasionally, if Sam's dinner especially excites him, he'll throw it up in the air, catch and hold it captive with his foot, and tear it apart with his teeth. This is an instinctive hunting habit that is characteristic of cats.

As I mentioned before, sometimes Sam requests to be petted while he eats. He conveys this message by leaning over his bowl and staring at one of us until we reach down and pet him. The contact inspires him to eat and brings him fond memories of the warmth and comfort he experienced in nursing. Because Sam is such a finicky eater, we try to indulge his whims. As he has grown older, he's become very frail. Baggins, on the contrary, makes up for Sam's svelteness. His build is ideal for construction or weight lifting and he has no intention of changing his image.

If you have a cat who, like Baggins, is a food addict, try to divert him when he screams for food out of turn. You can't feed him every time he's anxious and cries for food or he'll incorporate it into his habits and you'll have one very fat cat. As with Sam and Baggins, it is difficult if you're trying to encourage one cat to eat more, and the other to eat less. The chubby cat becomes upset and wants to eat even more as you encourage the skinny cat to eat on. Then you must find games and other diversions to attract the chubby one's attention and to show him you care. Don't be lazy and use food to fill the empty feeling in his gut when love and attention would fill the void. Give him attention in a serious and positive way or your chubby cat will eat even more.

Cats have many different eating patterns. They don't hesitate to communicate exactly what they want and what they *don't* want.

Has your cat ever scratched around his bowl as if he were trying to bury it? Either the food is spoiled or he wants another kind; his burying motion lets you know he wants the food removed from his sight. Generally, he'll continue this behavior until your attention is attracted and you do something about the food. If you're not around, he'll try to cover his dish with the closest possible object. When one of our hospital patients was unhappy with the cuisine, he often covered his dish with one of his towels. His nurse then supplied him with a new choice of food and a clean towel.

Although an older cat will often allow a kitten that has grown up with him to eat first (as with Sam and Baggins), this is not necessarily characteristic of grown cats introduced to each other as adults, even if one is a few years younger. In a multiple-cat household, it's usually every cat for himself. There may be exceptions, but the competition does not lend itself to bringing out altruistic tendencies in cats.

Often in multiple-cat households, some cats prefer to eat away from the others. There are six cats at the Eighth Street Bookshop in Greenwich Village. These include Otis, the mother; her four female offspring; and another male cat. When her kids were kittens, Otis was a devoted mother, but now two years later, she prefers to eat her meals in privacy. Why not—her kittens are now mature cats and there's even a male to play the heavy.

My friend, Ed, has to monitor the meals of his six cats. The four nibblers have to eat separately from Elvira and Boy, who tend to inhale their food and any other food around.

If you've ever lived with an ex-street cat, his ravenous appetite might, at first, have you amazed. A street cat has learned that he

can never really be sure of his next meal so he usually devours whatever is put before him. It takes many months of comfortable, domesticated living for a street cat to alter his eating patterns. When this change occurs, it's his way of expressing that at long last, he feels secure and won't have to be on the run again.

The eating relationship between a mother cat and her kittens is determined by the mother's source of food supply. If she's a house cat and doesn't have to hunt or scavenge in the streets for food, she's constantly available to nurse her kittens. If she's a street cat, however, she must search for her food before she can effectively provide milk for her kittens. Her supply of milk depends upon her health and her food intake. Sometimes the mother's milk will dry up before her kittens are old enough to be weaned, and her kittens may still go through the nursing motions. If this happens, the kittens' diet should be supplemented with a gruel of water mixed with canned food or baby food until the kittens are eight weeks old. At that time they can eat solid food.

When it comes to feeding kittens, it's best to put down a large bowl of food or separate bowls and try to keep them from climbing into the food. You may have to supervise to make sure the shyest kitten isn't pushed away by the hustlers. There isn't any special code that kittens observe. The most dominant or aggressive kitten gets the pick of the food.

A cat's physical and emotional state is heavily dependent upon his diet. A poor diet can cause a cat's fur coat to become dull and brittle. A cat will take less pride in grooming himself. It can also cause many other problems.

The Redwood Brothers were two mature Persians whose diet consisted mainly of tuna, canned meat, and dry food. They showed little interest in grooming themselves or each other and therefore needed constant, tedious, time-consuming combing and grooming because their fur was always matted. After they were put on a balanced diet, their fur started to look better and it rarely matted. Simultaneously, the Redwood cats began preening each other and it was apparent to their people that they looked and felt better.

Peaches was a shy four-year-old cat who had suffered several urinary attacks. Although emotional stress triggered the attacks, he was on a tuna and dry food diet that irritated his bladder and aggravated his problem. Part of the treatment was to start him on a proper diet which eliminated the previous foods. In time his person noticed that Peaches was more relaxed and outgoing.

A poorly balanced diet can often trigger skin disorders and aggressive or hostile behavior. Brownie is a one-year-old male who tore away at his skin and would frequently lash out at his people. Tuna fish was all he would eat. He was strictly a tuna fish "junkie." Brownie's treatment consisted of medication and a well-balanced diet that was very gradually added to his tuna until finally tuna was eliminated. Both Brownie's skin and temperament benefited by the change.

Tuna can cause a vitamin E deficiency in cats which manifests itself in skin problems, lethargy, frequent loss of appetite, and aggressive and/or nervous personality structures. Just because a cat shows a strong or exclusive preference for fish or dry food does not mean that he has made the right choice. There are children and even adults who would prefer to limit their diet to ice cream and other refreshments.

A cat is basically a carnivore and if left to his own resources, he will hunt for his food. He generally eats all of his catch, which provides him with his necessary food requirements. A domestic cat should be fed primarily beef and poultry. It can be fresh food that is cooked, or canned cat food. Cat food that contains meat or meat byproducts should be avoided because it contains low-quality ingredients that can cause allergic disorders. Cat foods that contain horse meat can trigger allergic problems.

Liver and other organ meats may be included in the cat's diet; table scraps are ideal. A combined teaspoon of brewer's yeast and wheat germ can be mixed into the food for extra vitamins. Some cats enjoy treats such as melon, yogurt, cheese, and pitless olives. Dry and semimoist food provide a good snack. Tuna and other kinds of fish can be fed to your cat occasionally, as long as he doesn't have any of the described problems. Boiled chicken necks and backs are an excellent source of exercise for the teeth. If your cat is a milk fan, but milk gives him diarrhea, cream is the answer.

If your cat enjoys catnip, you can give it to him on the floor or next to his bowl. Catnip is not a food but a plant of the clover family which seems to produce its unusual effect on cats from an estrogen-like substance in its leaves. Kittens usually have to mature before they can appreciate catnip, and there are cats who are indifferent to its appeal. But for many cats, catnip is a great treat. Some cats need only a small whiff to get them to roll around, run around, and to work off that pent-up energy. It may even cause them to sneeze and drool. Other cats prefer to devour the catnip and may not show any great energy outburst; but soon they're happily stretched out limply with a look of heavenly happiness on their faces.

Pretty Face is an adult cat who "arranged" his own private catnip stash. His people had often given him catnip on the terrace. Now and then, they'd notice him nibbling away at a plant in the garden. It wasn't until one day they found him sprawled out by the chewed off plant that they realized what had happened. Some of the seeds from the catnip had blown into the garden, bloomed, and presented Pretty Face with his own fresh catnip plant.

Electric is a cat who stood in front of the cabinet where his catnip was kept when he was in the mood for a nip. If his person tried to ignore him, he meowed and stretched his long body up the height of the cabinet. After he had enjoyed his nip, his look of happiness was always worth the trouble of fetching it for him.

Harpo is a fourteen-year-old cat who lives with his person, Bobby, and two younger companion cats, Motor and Razzle, and dog Nathan. Although age has enhanced Harpo's wisdom, it's slowed him down physically and he usually doesn't compete with his companions. But when catnip appears, Harpo's right up front for the choice of the nip. After he's had his fill of rolling and sniffing and acting like a kitten, Motor and Razzle partake in the catnip and Nathan supervises. But only after Harpo's completely indulged himself, do his companions come forth.

Catnip is one of the few attractions that can cause a cat to temporarily violate his dignity. Brandy lived at a local liquor store, and although he could be sociable, he projected aloofness.

But Brandy's aloofness vanished whenever I appeared with catnip. Not only did he try to snatch the container out of my hand as I sprinkled the catnip on the floor, but he pretended it was nonexistent so I had to keep sprinkling more and more. When I hit the right amount, Brandy completely forgot his sophistication, dived into the nip, rubbed his head from side to side, and danced a powerful shimmy. Since I'm only a social drinker my visits to Brandy's store were not too frequent, but they were certainly memorable.

There are different varieties of catnip but usually the most potent are homegrown from catnip seeds or bought from herb stores. Felix of Seattle, Washington offers potent kitty snuff that you can order by mail.

Some cats inhale their food as they eat. This habit can cause digestive problems. Kitty-Cat and Gray-Puss were mature cats that were fed twice a day. Both cats devoured their food almost instantly as soon as it was served. Kitty vomited periodically and her people couldn't figure out what was wrong. I advised them to increase her number of feedings to three a day. Kitty's vomiting was her digestive tract's signal that it was being overworked. By decreasing the amount of food given at any one time, Kitty's rapid eating would be less likely to cause her to vomit.

It's best to divide your cat's feedings into two or three meals a day. This can prevent future digestive problems in his senior years, especially if he is a fast eater. A kitten up to the age of eight weeks should be fed at least four times a day. He requires about one to one and one-half, six to seven ounce cans of food daily. After a cat reaches nine months, he should be fed about one can a day. However, let his body be your best judge. If he's chubby, feed him less; if he's too slim, feed him more.

If a kitten wasn't orally gratified enough during his nursing time, it's not unusual for him to develop an oral fixation, so that not only does he suck and lick material, but he lives to eat.

Sox and Tux were litter mates who were separated from their

mother when they were four and one-half weeks old. Sox had a sucking fetish and would suck on blankets, etc., whenever she became aroused. I suggested that their person distract Sox with a special piece of material whenever she began to suck. This way Sox might seek her special piece whenever she had the urge.

Kismet was a spayed female cat who actually devoured clothing and towels when she was anxious or aroused. When her people found her, she was terrified, undernourished, and pregnant; but it was safe to abort and spay her at the same time. She might not have survived a litter of kittens. Kismet got along with her three other cat companions but her residual anxiety caused her to become overstimulated and nip away at her people. I told Kismet's people that her anxiety was a result of her life experience before she met them. To Kismet, oral gratification—eating and nipping—was how she coped. I explained that with long-term reassurance and approval she'd begin to feel more secure. I recommended she be started on a tranquilizer as an auxiliary support.

The next time I spoke to Kismet's people, they reported that she appeared to have a better grip on the world. She no longer included them in her biting but still chomped away on their bathroom towels. In fact, they'd given Kismet her own private towel to snack on.

I explained that Kismet was especially attracted to their towels because of their body smells, but as her stress tolerance increased, her personality would become integrated to a point where she wouldn't be so orally aroused. As she became stronger, her sedation could be lowered and tapered off. In the meantime, catnip would also help her to work out her extra energy. I recommended that her daily feedings be increased so she would get the feeling she was being fed more.

Franklin was a mature cat that drove his people frantic with his insatiable appetite. His people had to divert him from the kitchen when he reached his daily food quota. This wasn't easy because Franklin was an expert food-snatcher. Melon was added to his diet because it was filling but low in calories. An adopted kitten would have been the perfect diversion, but Franklin's mental health couldn't cope with the competition of another cat.

Wake was a young cat who was another food-snatcher. He devoured his food and then tried to polish off Papillon's, his companion, who was a nibbler. Their person tried putting Papillon's food on an out-of-reach shelf, but then she discovered Wake could still find it. Now Papillon's dish is kept in a cabinet until her next nibble.

Cats can be remarkable when it comes to letting their people know which foods they need. Thomas's person was curious about his craving for vegetables, namely broccoli and beans. When it occurred to her that these were an excellent source of vitamin C, she understood Thomas's craving. Because of a chronic urinary problem, Thomas needs a daily dose of vitamin C. Whether instinctively or accidentally, he was attracted to the natural source.

Some cats have bizarre food passions and convey their desire in no uncertain terms. Teddy is a cat that's mad about taco chips, preferably with cheese and garlic. He actually snatches them out

of his person's hand or grabs them out of the bag. Pancake is a lettuce "freak." She once dashed off with a Bibb lettuce intended for a luncheon salad for visiting guests.

Donald Jr., a former resident, used to be mad about cinnamon Danish pastry. One afternoon while I was busy brewing tea, he was busy tearing into the Danish bag. We found him chewing away happily at a cinnamon Danish. Out of his good nature, he left the rest of the Danish for us. From then on, whenever we bought Danish, we presented Donald Jr. with his favorite. A word to the wise was sufficient.

Sigmund, Jenny, and Cassandra are wild about banana pancakes—but only smothered with strawberry jam. Where food is concerned, Skimby and Juan are like Jekyll and Hyde. Their person, Linda, tells us that they'll eat nothing but deli cold cuts. But when she's away, their cat sitter feeds them cat food, which they gobble up.

There are many cats who are dry-food addicts and will stop at nothing to get at these crunchies. Subway, Suzie, and Chi Chi used to drive their person, Barney, cuckoo with their crunchie-snatching tactics. No cabinet was safe from their raccoon-like clutches. One day Barney walked into the kitchen and the three of them were chomping away at wall-to-wall, spilled-out crunchies. Barney finally outlawed the raids by keeping the dry food package in the refrigerator.

Cats frequently like to be near their people when they snack. Debby is an adult cat who will carry her crunchies, one by one, and pile them up by her person's chair. While her person writes away at her desk, Debby snacks away at her crunchies.

At bedtime our cat, Sam, occasionally carts his crunchies from the kitchen to the bed. It could be that he feels if we eat Sunday breakfast in bed, he has a perfect right to enjoy his evening snacks there, too. The only problem is that Sam very often leaves his crumbs where they are a perfect target for us to roll on. By this behavior both Sam and Debby are saying that their crunchies make them happy and that they want to share their happiness with their people.

Occasionally, a cat can take on his person's food quirks. My friend Cindy's cat, Spy, used to demand to be included in Cindy's various food fetishes. Cindy would latch onto a certain food snack when she was under tension or had a heavy schedule. Spy, perhaps in sympathy with her or wanting to be part of the action, always followed her lead.

Biali was a mature male cat who had a remarkably touching food habit. When his cat companion was critically sick with cancer and too weak to eat, Biali used to chew extra food and put it into her mouth. This was exquisite devotion on his part.

A cat's state of being is deeply affected by what he eats. The same is true for all living things. If a cat's diet is not well balanced, eventually his health—physical and emotional—will reflect the nutritional stress. Combine the food information I've outlined to interpret your cat's food requests, and his eating patterns will be enhanced. Only remember: you mustn't believe that *everything* your cat desires is what he actually needs. Baggins is *always* my best friend whenever mealtime is near or I'm in the kitchen. If I obeyed all his food demands, he'd be six times bigger than Sam, instead of only three times bigger!

9.

TOILET HABITS

It was nine o'clock at night in a motel room in Columbus, Ohio, and the kitty litter bag was empty. Running out of litter in New York City is remedied by a quick trip to the corner store; however, things weren't quite as easy in Columbus—or at least, not in the area where we were staying.

I was in Columbus accompanied by Paul, Sam, and Baggins to make a publicity appearance for my book, *The Inner Cat.* We had miscalculated our litter supply and this could mean trouble. The only solution was to line the litterbox with strips of newspaper and hope that Sam and Baggins would go along with the change.

Well, we didn't have to wonder long. Baggins sauntered into the bathroom, stared first at the box and then at me as if to say, "You've got to be kidding!" I stared right back at him and told him it was just a temporary inconvenience and that there would be "real litter" in the morning. Baggins had no idea what I was saying but talking made me feel better. Anyway, the tone of my voice carried a ring of promise and confidence to help assure and relax him. I'm not sure what it was that motivated Baggins, but he did condescend to relieve himself in the box and I immediately cleaned up after him. By morning Sam had also visited the box. Perhaps it was in utter desperation that they responded, but whatever it was, we were thankful they chose to be adaptable. When it comes to toilet habits, Baggins is anal-compulsive, so he really went out of his way to stoop to paper.

Kitty litter was first on our agenda the next morning. I very quickly filled the box with litter and Sam very quickly christened it. Baggins followed Sam—that is, as soon as I'd scooped out Sam's deposit. Baggins would never mix his deposit with Sam's as long as he had us around. He was used to us scooping the box after each visit if we were in the vicinity. And after their great concession, Baggins certainly called the shots.

Sam is also particular but not as compulsive. Baggins will do everything but stand on his tail to call our attention to scooping out the dirty box before he has to use it, even between his own visits. Sam is more diplomatic. His strategy is to frequently coordinate "his business" with ours. Either he becomes stimulated by our activity or he likes company.

There are some house cats that won't object to a dirty box unless it becomes totally outrageous. I attribute this tolerance to

the standard of tidiness to which the cat has been accustomed. If the cat's person or people are slow in scooping or cleaning the litterbox, the cat is not as particular or demanding. Because I have a very sensitive nose and tend to be a do-it-right-away type, I'm sure I've contributed to and reinforced Baggins's fastidious nature.

Although an outdoor cat will instinctively seek a clean spot to bury his business, a house cat's toilet habits are definitely influenced by his person's attentiveness. I do think that we have overindulged Baggins's litter-sense; but there is a bottom line. A cat shouldn't have to seek out the rug or tub because his litterbox is too wet and/or full for him to feel comfortable in it. Don't encourage your cat to make life harder for you—you don't need such subtle reminders. Scoop the debris frequently and wash out the litterbox at least once a week to rid the box of any permeating odors.

It's not unusual for cats to be possessive about their bowel movements. P.C. was a kitten whose person was too quick to scoop. If she happened to be near his box when he left a deposit, she immediately scooped it out. P.C. was totally confused; he scratched and scratched away at the litter searching for his deposit. I told his person to wait a little longer in the future. A cat usually likes to do the initial cleanup. Even if he's aware of your assistance, his one-track mind will go offtrack unless you give him time to carry out his cleanup.

Do you have a cat who rarely buries his deposit? This is not a common behavior pattern but some cats just can't be bothered. I attribute this to a lack of energy or plain indifference. If it's an occasional happening, it may be because your cat is not feeling well.

It's convenient when a companion can assist a nonburier. Camille's toilet habits were always a source of complaining for her people. Because she never covered her debris, the scents really permeated their studio apartment. Conditions improved when they adopted Tabby, a four-month-old kitten. Each time Camille used the box, Tabby would run in after her and cover up. It may be Tabby's way of saying that Camille's indifference embarrassed her, or maybe she simply liked to clean up!

Preferences exist regarding different types of litters. Sam and Baggins prefer clay. Once or twice we tried litter with chlorophyll, and their reaction was both enlightening and amusing. Sam stared and sniffed at the litter, and jumped into the box in haste. He relieved himself and barely covered his deposit, which is very unlike him. Baggins circled the box a few times and almost turned up his nose before he actually used the box. When we found a pile of litter on the floor, we knew Baggins had revolted in no uncertain words. I can't say we were displeased with their preference. I found the smell of moist chlorophyll quite obnoxious. We're now a committed "clay" family.

Cats that are used to toileting outdoors will often go out of their way to avoid using a litterbox. Zelnik was a mature cat who grew up in the suburban streets. She spent most of her day outdoors but also enjoyed the comforts of home. One winter day the snow was coming down nonstop. Zelnik finished her breakfast and went over to her cat door as she did every morning. But it was closed. Her people had closed her cat door because this was no day for a cat walk! Zelnik had other ideas. She scratched away until someone opened the door for her. Very quickly, she darted outside, left her deposit, made a hasty retreat through her cat door, and spent the rest of the morning cuddled up in her basket by the radiator.

Kittens that are raised indoors but have an outdoor-going mother may become confused about their toilet habits. Scruffy was a three-year-old female that, without invitation, moved into an artist's country studio. Three days later she presented him with six kittens. Although the artist provided Scruffy with a litter pan, she avoided it and chose the outdoors. The artist knew that Scruffy would take care of her kittens' wastes until a certain age, but he wondered what they'd do on their own. He didn't want to let them go outdoors with Scruffy because he had found homes for them with various friends in the city.

I advised him to keep Scruffy indoors for a couple of days in a confined area with her kittens and litterbox. If Scruffy had no other alternative, she'd use the box and the kittens would follow her example. Normally, kittens will instinctively use a litterbox. However, Scruffy's avoidance of the litterbox could have been passed on to them.

Parasite problems and/or a new environment may cause a kitten to leave deposits outside his litterbox. Monkey is a six-week-old kitten who was adopted from a pet shop. He arrived in his new home with a severe case of diarrhea and left his deposits on exhibition on the sofa. His person took him to the vet who gave him some medication to settle his stomach and treat his worms. Monkey's diarrhea stopped but he still avoided the litterbox. His person was beside herself when she brought Monkey to see me. She knew she couldn't take him back to the pet shop and be able to sleep at night, but neither could she cope with "sofa detail."

One look at Monkey and I could see he was probably the runt of his litter. Not only had he been taken away from his mother too soon, but he was very underdeveloped for his age. Although his medication controlled his diarrhea, Monkey was very confused and disoriented by his new surroundings. I told his person to keep Monkey in a small, confined area with his food and litterbox. Now that his stomach was better, it would be easy for him to go right to his litterbox, if it were accessible. There'd be no chance for him to become confused and park his deposit on the sofa. When a cat has stomach and/or intestinal problems, he will quite often ignore his box to let his person know that he's uncomfortable. Although Monkey's medical problem had been treated, he probably was still bewildered by his change of environment.

The next evening, Monkey's person called to tell me that Monkey now seemed to feel at home. She followed my instructions and Monkey used his box like a champ. I told his person to keep this plan active for a few more days until Monkey's litterbox habits were totally reinforced.

Other parasite problems can cause a cat to reject his litterbox. (Infrequently, a cat may reject his litterbox because of a heart or chest problem.) Melody was a former resident cat that preferred the exam room plant garden to her litterbox. True, her deposits were good fertilizer but the scent was negative. It wasn't until one of the nurses reported seeing a ricelike substance in her stool that we realized she had tapeworm. We started her on medication and kept her out of the exam room for a couple of weeks so she wouldn't return to the scene of her crime.

Frequently, a cat will defecate outside his box for what appears to be no reason. This happened, as I mentioned earlier, with our cat Baggins. Although his box was clean and the brand of litter was to his liking, Baggins continued to go in the tub. Many stool specimens later, coccidia was isolated. Baggins's message was finally understood and we were able to start him on the right medication to treat his problem.

Anxiety can also cause a cat to forget his toilet training. Jefferson was another former resident cat who periodically avoided the litterbox. His "specimen spot" was the waiting room rug. Jefferson wanted everyone to receive his message! His stool samples were negative, but we decided to treat his behavior symptomatically and medicated him for various parasites. Then Jefferson began to use the litterbox, although he soon returned to using the rug. I realized that there had to be another reason besides parasites for Jefferson's bizarre behavior.

It then occurred to me that since Jefferson's personality was hypersensitive and was vulnerable to any kind of sudden noises or surprises, anxiety could be triggering his accidents. Jefferson was an ex-street cat, so his past was his own; there was no way to know for sure what made him so anxious. However, his stress target was his rectum and when he became anxiety-ridden, a spasm in his rectum was triggered and he defecated outside his box to draw our attention to his discomfort. We started him on a tranquilizer to relieve his anxiety and moved him to another part of the hospital so the rug wouldn't be a temptation. We had the rug thoroughly shampooed to rid it of any permeating odor that might stimulate Jefferson's memory.

The tranquilizer gave Jefferson the extra support he needed to cope. A few weeks later he was much more relaxed. Several weeks later he was off the medication and "on" his litterbox.

Environmental anxiety can affect a cat's toilet habits. C.J. was a young spayed female who moved with her person and companion cat into an apartment with three other cats and their person. C.J. kept to herself; she also kept away from the litterbox. She had defecated several times outside the box when her person called me.

Upon visiting C.J. and reviewing her case history, I observed that she was very nervous and anxious. She'd experienced a stressful kittenhood which explained her personality. I told her person to give her lots of positive support and it might be necessary to start her on a tranquilizer to relieve her anxiety. C.J. seemed to be intimidated by the other cats and their person, which caused a spasm in her rectum; so she avoided the box to convey her discomfort.

Her person called a few weeks later to report that she and C.J. had moved back home where she and her companion were the only two cats and C.J.'s toilet habits were normal again.

Our cat, Sam, has a rather extraordinary habit. I first caught his act when he was a young kitten; I thought he was doing the shimmy. He had just used his litterbox and strolled into the bedroom. There, he licked away at the base of his tail and then carefully dragged his rear across the rug. (Sometimes cats do this to indicate gland discomfort.) But it wasn't the shimmy that Sam was doing! He was using the rug to blot his rear. Then and now, toilet paper is out of the question. Sometimes he uses the bedspread if he's not in the mood for the rug. Luckily, he cleans himself well so there's rarely a trace on the rug or spread.

Sam also has another toilet habit that at first had me annoyed. One day I found a piece of stool on the bedroom floor and figured that Baggins was the culprit. I knew it was pointless to waste my breath, because I hadn't caught him in the act nor was I positive it was him. But I let him have a few choice words anyway. Of course, he appeared guilty and upset, but he was only reacting to the angry tone of my voice and my tense body.

The next day as I walked into the bathroom, Sam came tearing out, madly dragging his rear across the floor. This time, a piece of stool dropped off behind him. I started to shout at him, but then I realized what had happened. His stool was exceptionally hard and he wasn't able to completely pass it through in the litterbox. What appeared as extreme hysteria to me was Sam's way of passing the hard stool. Well, Sam's message was not in vain. For the next few days we added a commercial laxative to his food and made sure he got his share of butter from our bran muffins and bagels. Between the laxative and the butter, Sam's stool was back to normal very shortly. Now we make sure Sam's stools stay soft and we brush Sam and Baggins often so the hair they ingest from their grooming doesn't add to Sam's problem.

There are some commercial products that have a laxative effect that aids in hair removal. Bulk laxatives such as Siblin or Metamucil can be added to the food. Gel forms, such as Laxatone, Kat-lax, etc, can be licked straight from the tube. Fitzy is a cat who eagerly awaits his daily pills because his people coat them with the gel.

Constipation associated with a urinary problem will aggravate the situation. Linus was a four-year-old neutered male who had been treated for chronic urinary and constipation problems. Although he had a urethrostomy, which is a surgical procedure to widen the urinary passage and ease the urine flow, he still had periodic constipation. This seemed to cause him discomfort when he urinated. His people, Pat and Steve, brought him to see me because he seemed very unhappy and was interacting poorly with their other cats. Linus was still recovering from his surgery and had to wear a large collar so he wouldn't tear out his sutures. He was also kept apart from his companions at night because his people were afraid he'd fall down the stairs. This undoubtedly added to his unhappiness.

Linus was adopted from a pet shop and was their fifth cat. Usually, Samson, their fourth cat, was his best buddy. Pat and Steve were especially concerned because, although Linus was on a maintenance dosage of laxative, his constipation was acting up more frequently and his urine stream wasn't flowing easily. To add to Linus's emotional stress, one of their cats had passed away recently from leukemia. Linus and the other cats were negative for the virus, but the related anxiety also contributed to his condition.

As I wrote down Linus's case history, it became more and more apparent to me why Linus was such an anxious and insecure cat. My memories of his behavior when we hospitalized him for surgery also reinforced my impressions. He needed constant contact and attention, and it was evident that his self-esteem was not high. I explained to Pat and Steve that when Linus became anxious, he internalized his anxiety; his stress targets were his bladder and rectum. The tenser he became, the more he held in, the more his constipation built up and his bladder was affected. Lately, Pat and Steve had worked overtime and Linus was feeling neglected, which aggravated his condition.

I recommended that they allow Linus's buddy, Samson, to stay with him at night to keep him company, so he wouldn't feel totally rejected. Once his collar came off, their bedroom wouldn't have to be "off limits." Perhaps they could have a neighbor's child come in a few afternoons to give Linus extra attention. Linus had been given a tranquilizer before and I suggested they start him on one again to help relieve his anxiety. The combination of giving him extra emotional support as his primary aid, and a tranquilizer and increased laxative medication as his auxiliary aids, would give him the boost he needed. When his stress tolerance increased to a point where he felt better inside and his bladder and rectum were not such vulnerable targets, his medication could be tapered off and finally decreased.

Several months later Linus was off his medication. But I advised his people to keep him on a maintenance dosage of his laxative medicine and to give him a tranquilizer whenever they anticipated an anxiety-provoking situation. Because they were sensitive to Linus's feelings, they were able to interpret his discomfort and Linus's problems have been treated and arrested.

Sometimes a cat may suffer a physical injury to his pelvis that can cause him to have difficulty defecating. If laxatives are not effective, the cat's rectum may have to be emptied manually by the vet. Misty was a twenty-year-old cat who injured her pelvis in her early years. For a while, large doses of laxatives kept her regular, but for the past few years she had to be emptied manually once a week. She was a tough customer to handle, and both she and Paul were equally happy at the end of each clean-out.

In some cases the cat's person can give him assistance. Bombadille was a mature cat that also had suffered a pelvic injury. Unlike Misty, the injury also involved his spine so he had some motor difficulty. Once or twice a day his person pressed his abdomen. Without this assistance, Bombadille would be totally incontinent.

Misty and Bombadille's people cared enough not to begrudge the extra time and inconvenience their cat's disability caused them.

A well-balanced diet, frequent grooming, and minimum stress will aid your cat's regularity. If your cat's stool tends to be hard, milk or butter will help to soften it or you can use commercially made laxatives. If his stool is soft, try giving him cheese, rice, or pasta. If your cat tends to have regularity problems, keep in mind that stress-provoking situations may trigger attacks.

I understand why people become so upset when their cat refuses to urinate in his litterbox. Almost always the cat's person feels that his cat is doing it just for spite. Generally, they proceed to yell at their cat or try to discipline him—to no avail. A cat is an instinctively fastidious creature. Unless he is sick or a victim of the city streets and their elements, he takes pride in his appearance, and his toilet habits are faultless. When a cat goes to the trouble of choosing to urinate outside his box, there's a definite message he is trying to communicate to his person.

The arrival of sexual maturity is one reason a cat may avoid his litterbox. Georgie is an eight-month-old cat who lives with his companion, Sammy, and their people, Ellen and Ken, in Covington, Kentucky. While Ellen was interviewing me about my latest book, she told me about Georgie. Within the past few weeks he'd taken an occasional fancy to "decorating" areas other than his box. Otherwise, his behavior was about the same. I asked Ellen if Georgie played rougher with Sammy than before and if his urine smelled any stronger. Yes, was her reply to both. I told her that Georgie was reaching sexual maturity, leaving his kittenhood behind, and about to become a "cat." Ellen and Ken were surprised that Georgie had matured at such a young age. I explained that a male cat reaches sexual maturity anytime between five and fifteen months. A cat's behavior is usually a better indicator of his sexual maturity than his age.

As Georgie and Sammy swooned over the catnip toys I gave them, I noticed Georgie was quite "macho" in his interactions with Sammy. I recommended that they wait a week or so to make sure that Sammy's tomcat characteristics continued. If so, they should make an appointment with the vet to have him altered. If not, they could wait until his behavior became tomcattish again and then schedule surgery. A cat should be altered before he starts to spray outside the box, but his altering shouldn't take place until he is ready. (See Chapter 11 on Sex.)

Frequently, a cat will urinate outside of his box because of a medical problem. Although emotional stress may be one of the triggering forces, the medical problem must be treated before the cat's bizarre behavior will stop. If the source of stress can be determined, decreased, and/or eliminated, the cat's erratic behavior will sharply decline and soon stop.

Tilden is a three-year-old neutered male who suddenly started urinating indiscriminately around the house. His people were convinced that he did it when he was mad at them, to get their attention, and to get even.

In taking down his case history, it was apparent to me that there were a couple of factors that triggered Tilden's erratic behavior. His people had gone away on the summer weekends and left Tilden alone with an unlimited supply of dry food. New people had moved into an adjacent apartment with a tomcat which they allowed to roam the hall, and he frequently cried at Tilden's door. When this happened, Tilden cried back at him and was unusually anxious for the rest of the day.

I told Tilden's people that Tilden felt rejected when they went away. The emotional stress triggered a spasm in his bladder that caused him to strain and sometimes forget his toilet manners. The dry food contributed to the problem, and of course the tomcat next door was a major source of Tilden's anxiety. The tomcat's high energy level frustrated and annoyed Tilden. I recommended that they eliminate dry food from Tilden's diet; arrange for someone to come in twice a day when they went away weekends; and ask if the tomcat's people would have him altered, or at least kept out of the hall.

Tilden's urine was tested and although it tested negative, he was started on medication to relieve the spasm. Sometimes, despite the lack of any clinical signs, a cat can have cystitis, and should be treated symptomatically. Tilden's people were very cooperative and understanding. Several weeks later, Tilden was a "perfect shot"; he was off medication, the next-door cat was no longer a tom, and Tilden was off dry food. He had his own cat-sitter when his people went on holiday and there was a good chance he'd soon have his own adopted kitten. Yes, Tilden had been trying to get his people's attention, but for good reason.

Anastacia was a young, neutered cat who astounded her person, Joseph, when she took to urinating on his kitchen tile. Anastacia's problem turned out to be medical. A urinalysis revealed blood. Her standard x-rays were not remarkable but a pneumocystogram (i.e., an x-ray taken after air is injected into the bladder) showed the presence of bladder stones. Anastacia was scheduled for surgery and stones were removed. She soon transferred her business back to her litterbox.

Indiscriminate urinating is often precipitated by anxiety. In those instances a tranquilizer may be in order, in addition to positive people support. Sneakers is a three-year-old spayed female who lives with her companion cat and people. She had always been shy and nervous, and not particularly people-oriented. She interacted best with her companion cat. Sneakers was once treated for cystitis but otherwise her medical history was clean. The arrival of a newborn baby affected Sneakers dramatically. She avoided her litterbox and christened the baby's belongings with her urine. Although her urinalysis and other tests were negative, Sneakers was in discomfort. I explained to her people that Sneakers was threatened by the arrival of the baby. She couldn't cope with the baby's high energy level, so she became anxious. Her anxiety was transferred to her bladder, which is her stress target, and caused her bladder to go into spasm and ache. When this happened, she showed her discomfort by urinating on the baby's belongings because the baby was the source of her anxiety. I recommended that they try to give Sneakers extra attention, and start her on a tranquilizer to relieve her anxiety, and an antispasmodic to soothe her bladder. As her stress tolerance increased, her medication could be decreased slowly and tapered off. I also suggested they protect Sneakers from temptation by putting the baby's belongings out of reach.

Several days later Sneakers's people called to say that Sneakers was like a new cat. She was accepting their affection and even inviting it; her appetite had improved and she even joined them in bed. Best of all, she was using her litterbox again. Her medication was decreased over the next few months and, finally, given only in times of stress.

.

Sometimes a cat can have an undercurrent chronic problem in addition to a urinary disorder. Petrouchka was a mature, altered cat who was frequently treated for cystitis. It occurred to me that Petrouchka might have another problem that might aggravate his bladder problems. I remembered that when Petrouchka was hospitalized, his person mentioned Petrouchka had often strained when he used the litterbox, even as a small kitten. It struck me that he probably had a chronic ache that caused him to strain. X-rays of Petrouchka's bladder revealed a chronic arthritic condition in his hips, so antiinflammatory medication was added to his regimen. This stopped his straining, which helped to alleviate his cystitis.

REMEMBER: If your cat forgets his impeccable toilet habits, he's doing it to alert your attention. Whether it's a complaint about the condition of his box's sanitation, his coming of age, a medical problem, and/or an emotional problem that has triggered a medical disorder, time is of the essence in deciphering your cat's problem and finding the appropriate solution.

10.

BREATHING

As we hurried up the stairs to The Practice, I huffed and sighed away. We rushed over from home to check on Little Muggsy, a former resident cat that we had hospitalized for a severe spinal injury. He'd fallen from bed, and the fall jammed his spine and put pressure on the spinal cord in his neck region. His cervical vertebrae were already fused together and malformed from a former nutritional deficiency. Paul had put a brace around his neck to stabilize it.

Into the nursery I ran and there was Little Muggsy. He could hold up his head!! The brace had worked! Once again Little Muggsy had rallied.

As I tried to breathe a sigh of relief, I found that I momentarily couldn't get my breath to slow down; my chest felt like a jitterbugging gas pump. I'm not asthmatic but I could have passed for it. When I'm anxious I tend to hold my breath. In a stressful situation such as this, my body violently contracts, energy gets bottled up, and I gasp for a while until I calm down and my breathing can relax and flow freely. I try to remind myself not to hold my breath during moments of anxiety or conflict, but it's a long-cultivated habit and I must constantly work at it.

Long before I was fully aware of my own anxiety-related breathing patterns, I became aware that a cat's breathing is often an excellent barometer of his feelings and health. From observing so many cats, some healthy, some moderately sick, some critically ill, I observed various patterns in their breathing.

Rapid cat-breathing is caused by temporary stress. A trip in a cat carrier, a sudden surprise, exercise, or a chance in temperature causes a cat to breathe rapidly. But this is temporary and not prolonged.

When a cat has been subjected to constant, long-term stress, his body becomes tense, his muscles contract, and his breathing is compromised. He is more vulnerable to sickness and the weakest part of his body—his stress target—will be attacked. Many times emotional stress can trigger an overt asthmatic problem, and in this instance, there's a direct, obvious correlation between cause and effect. The stress triggers rapid breathing and bronchial spasms.

But sometimes an asthmatic problem can be insidious. The cat

109

appears to show no regular symptoms other than bizarre behavior. Columbia was a mature, spayed cat who suddenly became a late-night howler. Every evening she would scream to be let out into the apartment hall and would continue to scream nonstop until she was finally diverted. Her people said there hadn't been any change in Columbia's daily routine or environment. Although she had a varied medical history, which included skin problems, at present her medical slate was clean. As I studied Columbia's breathing, it appeared a bit rapid and I wondered if this wasn't the key to her howling.

X-rays revealed that Columbia was asthmatic. Columbia's way of communicating her breathing discomfort was to howl until she was noticed. Admittedly, it was a bizarre way to announce her discomfort, but probably her chest was most uncomfortable by the end of the day. The discomfort made her restless and anxious, and she tried to get away from her discomfort by focusing her attention on the hall. As she ran around, her breathing became more compromised. Her howls were the result of her anxiety and discomfort.

Columbia was started on antiinflammatory medication and a tranquilizer to relieve her anxiety. She had the "classic" personality structures for an asthmatic cat—she tended to be generally high-strung and sensitive. Columbia's varied past medical problems were stress factors that contributed greatly to her developing asthma because their frequency lowered her body's resistance.

Life can't exist without breath. The more comfortably your cat can breathe, the easier is his whole life process. For example, a cat may be born with a congenital cardiac defect that may or may not affect his breathing. If his breathing is irregular, his heart should be checked periodically. I've noticed various ex-street cats that have constant rapid breathing because of their stressful pasts, but no other side effects.

If your cat's breathing is noticeably irregular and you can't link it to a particular variable such as heat, excitement, or over-exercise, it's a good idea to have him checked out. His breath may be telling you something.

Quite frequently a cat's disorder can involve the interaction of two stress targets. Albert is a mature, neutered cat that frequently urinated on the bed. His bladder was uncomfortable but it was not his primary trouble source. It turned out to be his secondary stress target. His chest was his primary stress target —when he became anxious and overstressed, his breathing became rapid and triggered a bronchial spasm. This caused a chain reaction which affected his next vulnerable target—his bladder. Once he was started on medication for his asthma his bladder spasm was controlled, and his "bed affinity" disappeared. As his stress tolerance was increased with the support of special attention, comforting, and medication, his asthmatic attacks declined.

Timothy is another neutered male who was treated for a chronically severe urinary disorder. He was hospitalized and at one point, his condition became critical. At that time, it became apparent that his heart was his primary stress target. His heart muscle had become scarred and thickened. Timothy was started on medication for his heart and a tranquilizer to relieve anxiety. But it was still touch-and-go for a few days. Fortunately, with his family's strong support, lengthy visits, and medication, his bladder (which was his secondary target) stabilized and Timothy rallied. Several months later Timothy's heart medication and tranquilizer were maintained at a low level and his bladder was comfortable and relaxed. I told his people that whenever Timothy was overanxious or stressed, his heart would be taxed and they should anticipate by giving him extra attention and medication. They mentioned that they planned to move out of the city; I explained to them that this would be a major change for Timothy and the stress could cause him to have a relapse. To prevent such an occurrence, his medication would need to be increased to provide him with extra support. Again, he would need extra comforting, etc.

Another case comes to mind. Malcolm, a mature, neutered male, periodically urinated outside his litterbox. In reviewing his case history, I found out that he'd lived with a companion cat with whom he shared an amicable relationship. However, she was moved to another home because of their person's allergy. For a while, Malcolm was outwardly very lonesome and depressed, but in time, he recovered. I wondered, though, if his separation-anxiety hadn't triggered a medical problem. Although his breathing appeared normal, he had experienced a traumatic situation; x-rays of his bladder were normal but he *did* have a heart problem.

Further questioning revealed that Malcolm didn't actually avoid the box but had trouble positioning himself and making his target. This information indicated that his accidents were due to a general circulatory deficiency that caused temporary oxygen starvation to and cramping of his muscles when he strained to urinate. His person also mentioned that Malcolm had suffered a broken hind leg when he was a young cat. Malcolm's old injury contributed to his discomfort when he tried to position himself in his litterbox. He was started on medication for his heart, an antispasmodic for his bladder, and an antiinflammatory medication.

Several weeks later, Malcolm's incidents had almost disappeared and his person felt that when he was stabilized, they would get another cat. A new companion for Malcolm would help him to release his energy naturally and reduce anxiety-provoking situations that stressed his heart.

Albert, Timothy, and Malcolm all shared one common characteristic. Their urinary problems were triggered by an underlying source of distress. Stress was the activator. Until the source was identified and treated, their urinary problems acted up.

Skin problems can be triggered by heart trouble. Louie was a mature, neutered male that suffered chronic skin problems. His case history revealed several stressful experiences that made me suspect his skin was not the immediate source of discomfort.

Louie's breathing pattern (which was subtly irregular), also resembled that of a cat with heart trouble. X-rays confirmed my suspicion. He was started on medication. His fur grew back, so his medication was slowly tapered. Like Timothy and the others, I recommended that Louie's medication be increased in times of stress and that he be given positive support such as extra attention, treats, etc.

Albert was an eight-year-old, neutered cat who also had a chronic skin problem. He had the "creeping crud" foot disorder. His people carefully monitored his diet and provided him with constant positive support. His interaction with his companion cat, Hester, was amicable. But every time his medication was stopped or reduced to a low level, the skin on his feet became inflamed, oozy, and angry looking.

Again, I suspected there was an underlying cause. Although Albert was outwardly very mellow, his body posture and breathing suggested a heart problem. X-rays confirmed my theory, and Albert was started on medication. Within several weeks, his "creeping crud" healed and his future prognosis was very positive.

Although Louie and Albert's primary target was their heart, their diet still had to be monitored because they were highly susceptible to skin problems. There's a possibility that their hearts may grow strong enough so that medication may not be necessary.

Whiskey, a six-year-old, spayed female, was treated for chronic cystitis and convulsions. Until two years ago, she was her person's only cat and had many of the characteristics of the cat-friendless cat. She was very tense and unfriendly. Because of her insecurity, whenever she came for an appointment, she was very threatening. The addition of two new companions mellowed her outward behavior tremendously, but the internal damage was already initiated. Whiskey suffered a series of convulsive episodes that didn't respond to treatment. When she came in for a checkup I noted her rapid, irregular breathing.

She had a heart disease, which responded favorably to medication. Once her heart stabilized, Whiskey's other disorders declined or disappeared so she needed only supportive cardiac medication. The fewer stress-provoking situations such cats experience, the easier their hearts pump.

Most of these cats that had evident rapid breathing along with other factors in their particular case histories, caused me to suspect an asthmatic or cardiac condition. Their conditions were not critical, however.

Many of the cats I've worked with *did* have critical problems. Some could be made comfortable indefinitely, others temporarily, and there were those who were quickly nearing the end. My common observation with these cases was that their breathing pattern was very deep and rapid, and the more critical their condition, the more out-of-contact was the look in their eyes. Most cats with critical problems prefer not to be handled or comforted, and will withdraw. But there are others that choose contact to the end.

Billie was a mature, spayed female who had never had any remarkable problems. Her family brought her in for a checkup because she appeared uncomfortable and wasn't eating. One look at her breathing and eye contact and I knew Billie was in severe trouble. Her x-rays indicated a severe, irreversible heart condition. Medication could not give her the essential support to rally even temporarily. By that evening she was in great distress, but she still wanted her people near her. They brought her in and stayed with her as we assisted her end. That's the way Billie wanted it.

As I've mentioned in my introduction, I reported my observations of each cat's emotional makeup and behavior with my recommendations to Paul, and he applied the necessary and vital medical techniques. Diagnostic techniques or emotional observations alone are not enough. By collaborating on our individual findings, we were able to treat the total patient. Only then did we contribute the best of our souls.

Poor breathing patterns develop in all species as the body arms itself against real or perceived threat. As I've explained, the stress can be internal or external. But the outcome of these unresolved anxieties is often physical disease. The first step in dealing with these problems is to recognize the multiple factors involved. The second step is to devise a treatment plan that deals as adequately as possible with the initial symptoms. The third step is to realize that the treatment process may have to be adjusted a few times over before the problem is stabilized. Time, cooperation, and understanding will gradually allow the process to reach its ultimate effect.

11.

SEX

I could feel my body relax and my head unwind as I sat on the living room sofa and watched Sam and Baggins in their basket amongst the plants. Sam's look was of exquisite delight as Baggins wrapped his paws around him and washed his neck. By the way they breathed and moved their bodies to and fro, I knew they were both purring away.

Sam and Baggins are both neutered males. Their sensuality was not affected when they were neutered. I wished Gail, one of the people I'd advised that afternoon in Hartford, Connecticut, could get a gander at our two guys now. Gail has two unspayed females and hers was one of the house calls I made while being filmed for a local television show. Gail's cats, Long Cat and Snively, had eating problems. Snively wanted all the food for herself and lately both cats seemed uncomfortable. Gail couldn't figure out why Snively was such a chow-cat. She wondered if Snively were trying to relay some kind of message to her.

During my visit, her cats were very responsive and nestled beside me in spite of the intrusion of the television camera. They enjoyed contact but Snively especially, was a bit wired. Gail mentioned that they'd had their first heat this summer. In fact, Snively's heat had lasted all summer.

I explained to Gail that being unspayed was the key to their rivalry and discomfort. When a female cat reaches sexual maturity, she goes into heat. Unless she is bred, each time she has a heat, she won't ovulate, and the follicles in her ovaries can become cystic. This hormonal imbalance can sometimes trigger physical and personality disorders. Snively and Long Cat's sexual maturity had raised their energy level. However, the natural expression of this energy was stifled because they weren't mating. Snively was overactive and uncomfortable because she had had such a long heat period.

Gail mentioned that she had heard that cats become fat and lethargic when they were spayed, and wasn't it wise to let them each have at least one litter. I told Gail that a female cat usually becomes more relaxed after being spayed because she isn't charged with excess, unused energy. Since she's more relaxed, her metabolism may slow down. If this happens, her diet should be regulated so her food intake isn't any more than she actually needs. This applies especially to an indoor cat. Outdoor cats can exercise more. Allowing a female to have one litter doesn't necessarily improve her health or personality. Not every female cat has a burning maternal instinct. Sometimes people use this assumption to satisfy their own desire for kittens.

Gail asked if having her cats spayed would improve their relationship and stop the food rivalry. I told her that a few weeks after surgery, their hormone levels would diminish and Snively, especially, would feel and act calmer. No longer would she have that pent-up energy that she transformed into offensive and destructive behavior toward Long Cat. The surgery would relieve the mischanneled energy. I added that there was nothing to gain by putting off their surgery.

But Gail had one last concern. She was afraid her cats would lose their sensuality after they were spayed. I assured Gail that spaying her cats wouldn't make them nonsensual. This would happen only if they were spayed before they reached sexual maturity. (A female cat reaches sexual maturity between five and one-half and eleven months.) They had both been in heat already, which indicated they were sexually mature.

Cats don't intellectualize their sexuality. Their behavior is controlled by their highly developed senses; that is, cats feel things

117

out rather than think them out rationally. Because cats are mainly controlled by their feelings, they're more concerned with satisfying their needs in the most direct way possible. In contrast to people, cats' basic, instinctive feelings don't get modified and sometimes wiped out by intellect. Snively and Long Cat were already sexually mature; their hormones had triggered the area of their brains that controlled their femininity. A cat's sensuality is not dependent on his or her sex organs. Sometimes a cat will become even more affectionate and sensual after surgery because he or she feels emotionally and physically better.

That is why, as I sat and enjoyed the beautiful exhibition of Sam and Baggins caring for each other, I couldn't help wishing Gail could witness their interaction.

Unspayed cats and personality quirks remind me of Nightingale, a former resident cat. Nightingale was at least two years old when she made her debut at The Practice. Her personality was very low key and although Paul did not notice any abdominal scar to indicate a prior hysterectomy, rather than whisk her off to surgery for an exploratory, we decided to see if she displayed any telltale signs.

Nightingale, indeed, must've read our script. A month later she boycotted her litterbox and left her piles on the waiting room sofa. At first we thought she'd been locked in the waiting room. But after the second and third times, it was apparent she was going through a silent, but visibly active heat. Nightingale went to surgery the next day and Paul removed an abnormally large uterus and cystic ovaries. Her strategically placed piles were a result of the unspayed syndrome. It's not uncommon for an unspayed cat to forget her toilet training.

Unspayed females can transfer their frustrations to people as well as to companion cats. Auntie Mame is another former resident cat who arrived at The Practice unspayed. We were aware of Auntie's status because her person brought her in to be examined prior to spaying. She mentioned how Auntie Mame was very unpredictable. At times she was very affectionate. Other times she would lash out with her claws or give an unprovoked nip. Her person heard that getting Auntie spayed might regulate her disposition. I confirmed her information and Paul checked Auntie out as best he could above her hissing and striking out. Auntie's person was to pick her up in two days.

It's not uncommon for unspayed females to show hostile or aggressive behavior toward people. Their high energy level fosters anxiety, and they tend to direct their energy toward attacking the source of their anxiety. As far as Auntie Mame was concerned, we were the source of her anxiety; so we were her aggression target. Her person also appeared to be nervous and tense, so she was a natural target for Auntie's bestiality. Once Auntie was spayed, her anxiety level would decrease and she'd no longer be driven to attack to protect herself. Her person would really appreciate the change in Auntie.

Although Auntie was barely approachable, Paul was able to perform the surgery. She actually allowed us to comfort her a bit that evening, but she was still skeptical. But Auntie's person never showed up. When we were unable to contact her by phone, I sent one of our staff to her given address. But there was no such person in residence nor did the doorman recognize her description. Poor Auntie! Although she had started to relax, her anxiety would build again when she realized she wasn't going home. Her person was a true "love 'em and leave 'em" type!

That evening Auntie's body was as rigid as steel and she refused to eat. We started her on a tranquilizer to relieve her anxiety. The next morning she ate her breakfast and tolerated minimum contact. Several days later she was more receptive to contact but still hissed if she got excited. I wondered about Auntie's outcome. First the unspayed syndrome, and now she had nobody but us, and to her we were the bad guys. She was a very pretty cat with striking markings but her personality wasn't adoption-oriented.

Well, Auntie's luck changed dramatically when our friend

Sylvie came in with her new kitten. Sylvie mentioned that her kitten seemed lonely so I decided to show her Auntie Mame. Sylvie thought Auntie was beautiful, but she wasn't sure she could cope with another cat. The next day however, she called to tell us she couldn't get Auntie and her story out of her mind. How soon could she have her?

Auntie moved in with Sylvie and her kitten, Squeaky, that evening. I was a bit skeptical about Auntie's performance level but hoped the new kitten and Sylvie's good feeling would be her security blanket. Two days later Sylvie reported that Auntie and Squeaky were an "item." Auntie felt so secure and comfortable that she even slept with Sylvie and the kitten curled right up beside her. Auntie was on her way! No longer did she feel threatened and anxious. Surgery, a loving person, and her own kitten provided her with all the supportive therapy she needed.

Sometimes I think my recollection of problem-plagued, unspayed cats is endless. One of my clients came to me with her male cat, Sam, who was neutered and eight years old. He lived with his companion cats, Tina and Mousie. Although Tina, the younger female, was his favorite, he tolerated Mousie, who was more people-oriented. But recently Sam's behavior towards Mousie was intolerable. His person was afraid he might actually hurt her.

One look at Sam, and I could understand his person's apprehension. Such a big hulk of a cat and, no doubt, very self-possessed. He allowed me to pet him but by the feel of his body, I could tell Sam was on guard.

In taking down their history, I found that Mousie was spayed but Tina was intact. Her person didn't have Tina spayed because her heats were infrequent and low key; but it was Tina who was the source of Sam's anxiety.

I explained to Sam's person that Tina's high sexual energy triggered Sam's anxiety. But because Sam favored Tina, he transferred his hostility to Mousie. If Tina were spayed, Sam would stop victimizing Mousie. The longer Tina remained intact, the longer she would be uncomfortable, and Mousie would be on the losing side of the triangle. Mousie was an indirect victim of the unspayed syndrome. Sam's intolerable behavior should radically change once Tina was spayed—and it did.

When an unspayed cat has medical and emotional disorders, the situation can become critical. Recently, I received a call from an hysterical young lady who knew of me through my books. Her cat, Tara, had attacked one of her roommates, struck out at her; so Tara had to be taken to the hospital by ambulance. Because Tara was unapproachable, they had to anesthetize her so she could be examined and tested. The doctors told Tara's person they couldn't find anything medical to cause her hostile behavior, and because she'd attacked someone once before, they

recommended that Tara be put down. Marlene, Tara's person, didn't want Tara to be killed and she hoped that I could give her some advice.

Upon questioning Marlene, I found out that Tara was six years old, unspayed, and on medication for a chronic skin problem. Marlene had found Tara in Paris as a young kitten and shortly afterwards, Tara had been severely injured when she fell onto the subway tracks. Lately Marlene had been sleeping at a friend's and with her full-time job, she had little time for Tara.

I explained to Marlene that Tara was a victim of the unspayed syndrome and that her traumatic kittenhood had added to her present status. An unspayed cat has a high energy level and is generally more vulnerable to emotional stress, which can trigger medical problems. Tara's stress target was her skin. Marlene's recent absence from home threatened Tara's security. She became anxious and transferred her hostility to Marlene's roommate, holding her responsible for all of her grief. I strongly urged Marlene to have Tara spayed and to make an effort to spend more time with her. Tara was in dire need of reassurance and positive support. I also recommended that she be started on a tranquilizer to relieve her anxiety. She needed all the help she could get to help her cope.

Marlene decided to transfer Tara to The Cat Practice to have her spayed. Because she was unapproachable, she was anesthetized inside her carrier and then surgery was performed. In addition to her skin problem, Tara also had clogged anal glands and a severe case of ear mites. At last, all of her problems could be treated. I told Marlene that Tara would have to remain on a tranquilizer for several weeks. It then could be tapered slowly and eventually stopped. It would take a while for Tara's stress tolerance to increase to the point where she could function on a day-to-day basis without being easily threatened.

I paid a house call to Tara the day after her surgery. Her reaction to the tranquilizer was good. Although she moved very slowly and appeared quite sleepy, I could tell she wasn't anxious and she even allowed me to stroke her. The next day Marlene reported that Tara's confrontation with her roommates was remarkable. Tara surprised them all by climbing into the lap of the roommate she had attacked. I told Marlene that Tara's progress was very encouraging and her prognosis was excellent. However, when she wasn't home, she should enclose Tara in her room to make sure she didn't encounter any anxiety-ridden situations with her roommates. As Tara's confidence and security grew with Marlene's support and the help of the tranquilizer, Tara could be given more space. It was best for Tara to progress slowly so her personality would become well integrated on a long-term basis. Tara had experienced a great deal of emotional and medical stress, and it would take a while for her to recover.

A female cat can sometimes become "very" pregnant before her person gets the message. Spats, my sister Gail's cat, moved in two years ago with Gail and her cat Raggs. Gail's house is in Nichols Canyon, a section of Los Angeles. Raggs spends most of his day outdoors, which is where he met Spats. Gail met Spats when Spats started following Raggs into the house. She'd roam through the house but scamper through the cat door whenever Gail tried to go near her. She was truly a cat-oriented cat. She only had eyes for Raggs. Sometimes she'd show up for a few days in a row, but then she'd disappear for a while. Gail wasn't actively looking to adopt another cat but when Spats started hanging around day after day, Gail accepted the fact that Spats was the cat for Raggs.

Spats spent all of her day with Raggs but at night she began to crawl into Gail's bed. Raggs was there, too, but Gail was amazed when Spats actually rubbed up against her to be petted. I told Gail it was because she was relaxed, as most people are in bed; Spats didn't feel threatened and was able to accept and invite Gail's attention.

Months went by and Spats became a little more people-oriented, but she was still leery. Gail assumed she was already spayed because although she went outdoors and was free to mix with male cats, she didn't become pregnant. Raggs was altered, but there were other loose males around. In fact, Jaboo, a cat mentioned earlier, lived next door. (He was the one who ran away from home and moved in with people across the canyon.) Before Jaboo was altered and even after, he used to come over to visit Spats, but Raggs eventually chased him away. Oddly enough, Jaboo was the only male cat who blatantly came after Spats. It was almost as if he were aware of something that no one else was.

Gail mentioned that sometimes Spats rolled around the floor, shot her rear up in the air, made "goo goo" eyes at Raggs, and became very affectionate toward her. This was very out of character for Spats. When Gail told me this, I suggested that when she acted like this Spats might possibly be in heat, and it might be wise to have her vet do an exploratory. Well, Gail was working on a movie and time went on. She called one evening with some very momentous news. She had noticed that Spats was

putting on weight, so she had taken her to the vet, who announced that Spats was at least six weeks pregnant. Evidently, Spats was in heat whenever she surprised Gail with her "come-get-me" act. Jaboo sensed Spats was intact, which is why he had pursued her as well.

If Spats had been more people-oriented, chances are Gail wouldn't have put off taking her to the vet. If Spats had been already spayed, she probably wouldn't have been so skittish. It's mysterious why she didn't become pregnant sooner. But now, at least, Gail was aware of her status and Spats was spayed soon after her kittens were adopted. Jaboo was no dummy. He, if nobody else, was aware of Spats's condition.

As I stated earlier, the hormonal imbalance in an unspayed cat can trigger medical as well as emotional disorders.

Delilah was a six-year-old female who had two miscarriages before she was finally spayed two years ago. The emotional and physical stress lowered her resistance. Her initial target was her skin. She tore the hair off her belly. X-rays revealed an underlying cardiac problem. Medication, combined with love and understanding from her person, was her treatment. Delilah's response was positive and her medication was slowly tapered.

Often people don't bother to have their female cat spayed because she doesn't externalize her heat—by that I mean, the lower part of her body doesn't appear sensitive, she doesn't howl away or avoid her litterbox, her personality is on the mild side, and she isn't exposed to other cats. A female cat who doesn't externalize any signs of heat can internalize her anxiety and discomfort, which may, as she grows older, precipitate various medical problems. One common problem is that her uterus may get infected, a condition known as *pyometra*. The physical and emotional stress can make an unspayed female cat an ideal target for cancer. Usually the cancer shows up in the form of breast tumors. The cat's person feels lumps in her cat's breast and the vet diagnoses them as tumors, which are usually malignant. Treatment consists of either removing the tumor surgically or using medication in hope of controlling the situation. In either case, positive-support therapy from the cat's person is most essential to the cat's welfare. The prognosis depends on the severity of the tumors. Some cats can survive comfortably for months, others years, and there are those whose days are numbered. Even if a cat's heats are silent and there's no chance of her becoming pregnant, it's best to have her spayed when she's sexually mature rather than taking the chance of her developing a serious physical disorder. Don't wait for your cat's body to relate such alarming news.

The behavior and body language of an unaltered male or tomcat is usually most dramatic. The most common characteristics of the tomcat syndrome are on-again, off-again howling, a strong urine odor, indiscriminate urinating—better known as spraying—and a rough and tough personality.

A tomcat that goes outdoors is in a nonending state of stress. He constantly has to deal with other toms. If it's not a territorial brawl, it's a sexual brawl over a female in heat. A street tom's life span is limited. He's forever on the run. It's an endless quest for food, warmth, and sex. Often a tom on the run is hit by a car. As a tom's age increases, his potential for survival and conquering other toms decreases. But as long as he's a tom, he'll continue to battle and his body will show the scars.

Frequently, a male cat's person is totally surprised and confused when he comes of age. Studs was a ten-month-old male who lived with his person and companion cat Sinbad, who was neutered. His person called one day all worked up over Studs. For no apparent reason he'd started to bully and corner Sinbad. She couldn't figure out what had come over Studs! He'd been doing this for several days. She thought it was a passing fancy but each day Studs got more aggressive and today, he urinated outside his box.

Indeed, Studs had come of age! His person laughed when she realized what he was trying to say. She wasted no time and scheduled Studs for surgery. If she prolonged the surgery, she

would inadvertently reinforce Studs's negative behavior toward Sinbad.

It takes about two weeks after the surgery for a male's hormone level to decrease and his "macho" behavior to recede. Basil was a two-year-old cat who was adopted from a local shelter. He moved in with Tranquillo, a six-year-old, altered male with a very mellow personality. Tranquillo accepted Basil but their people were bewildered with Basil's "style." He would grab Tranquillo and roll around with him again and again until Tranquillo really seemed pooped and retreated to his food dish or basket. They remarked that their former cat, Silvester, had never tolerated Basil's guff; they wondered if he'd ever calm down.

Yes, Basil would calm down! He had been with them for less than two weeks and his scrotum indicated that he had been recently altered. Not to worry, Basil would eventually soften his style.

The presence of an alien tomcat may cause a cat to attack her companion cat. During my publicity tour in Chicago for my book *The Inner Cat,* I was interviewed by Mary Daniels, the author of *Morris.* She told me how a tomcat had showed up in her yard and her older cat, Mama Bear, went into a rage. The tomcat managed to escape her wrath, but Mama then transferred it to her companion cat, Ashley. Fortunately, Mary managed to distract Mama before she'd whacked Ashley too many times. She mentioned that Ashley's high energy level usually drove Mama to another room, so maybe it was his turn to absorb a hit. As Ashley whizzed around the living room and Mama headed toward the bedroom, I could see that he was a perpetual motion machine.

The next time I spoke to Mary she mentioned that Ashley had a new outlet for his high energy. When her daughter, Roxanne, babysat for the children next door, she took Ashley along and the kids gave him all the exercise he could handle.

Sometimes the arrival of a sexually mature male can affect an altered male's toilet habits. Tepee was a thirteen-year-old, altered male who started urinating around the house when a new male cat was introduced. I explained to Tepee's person that Tepee sensed the new male was coming of age. He couldn't cope with the male's high sexual energy level. The stress triggered a spasm in his bladder. As a result, he urinated outside the box to show his discomfort. The new male's presence distressed him and triggered a urinary problem. I recommended that Tepee be checked out by the vet, that the new male be altered if he was indeed sexually mature, and that the cats be separated until the situation was under control. An older, altered male cat can be stressed by a newcomer cat even if the newcomer hasn't reached sexual maturity. In any event, the older cat must be made to feel better before his problem will subside.

One client was totally flabbergasted when Spotty, her six-year-old, altered male, backed up against the screen door and sprayed. She mentioned that the male cat next door was over that morning running around the porch. I explained to Spotty's person that Spotty was protecting his territory and even though he was altered, he could spray when motivated. However, it probably wouldn't smell like a tomcat's spray because Spotty was

already altered. I suggested she find out if the neighbor's cat was intact and sexually mature. If so, perhaps he could be altered. Spotty's marking of territory would stop when he wasn't threatened by the male next door.

Skibam is an altered, snow-white male who lives at a furniture shop. Most of the time he may be found adorning one of the color-coordinated sofas where he's sure to be admired by the clientele. His favorite is the shop window where he's center stage. One day one of the staff dropped her shawl next to Skibam. She was flabbergasted when he jumped on it and sprayed away. For an altered cat his urine was potent; if he were a tom, it would've been curtains! As it was, Skibam had good reason for his demonstrative behavior: the staff girl's female cat had been in heat, and she had been lying on her shawl. Skibam was altered but still had a nose for a female in need!

One of my most urgent pleas for help with her male cat came from a lady in Texas. Her letter stated that she had found a male cat, Tiger, two months ago and had, at that time, taken him to the vet to be checked out. He was in good health and the vet told her he'd already been altered.

She recently adopted an adolescent female cat named Bubbles. Although Tiger accepted her, he'd sometimes jump on her and bite her neck. Before Bubbles arrived, Tiger's urine was strong, but now it was almost unbearable and her visitors were asking who the tomcat was. She wondered if Tiger was doing this for spite. Maybe he resented Bubbles.

Poor Tiger and poor lady! I quickly dashed off a letter to Tiger's person so she could immediately take action. In it I explained that Tiger was probably, in fact, still a tomcat and Bubbles's appearance triggered his tomcat behavior. When the vet examined Tiger, he didn't see any testicles, so he assumed Tiger was altered. Quite possibly, Tiger *was* altered, but with only one of his testicles removed. Sometimes one of a male's testicles does not descend and the vet routinely removes the one that has, but doesn't bother to take the time to look for the one that hasn't. A retained testicle will cause a male to display tomcat symptoms. I recommended that Tiger's person arrange to have her vet perform an exploratory to remove the lurking testicle.

Several days later, Tiger's person wrote back that Tiger was no longer a tom. An exploratory revealed the hidden testicle; it was removed and Tiger was recovering from his surgery with the help of all his favorite treats. Her house no longer smelled and Tiger was treating Bubbles nice and easy!

My friend, Phyllis, has an ongoing evening attraction presented by her cats, Barnaby and Tulip. Although they're both neutered, each evening is a "gala affair." Barnaby gives Tulip the old "once-over" look and she takes off toward the bedroom. He follows in hot pursuit and soon he has her by the neck and off they go. When Tulip's satisfied, she takes off, and the next night they continue where they left off. Phyllis couldn't understand how her two neutered cats could be such hot numbers. I explained to her that although a cat is neutered, he is still able to experience sexual sensations. If inclined, he can indulge in the motions. Evidently, Barnaby and Tulip were so inclined.

Chrissy and Mickey are two other neutered companion cats. Mickey still occasionally comes on like a tomcat with Chrissy. Sometimes she encourages him but other times she grabs him and gives him a good, strong whack.

Because a domestic cat does not live a pure, natural life, it is in his and his people's best interest to have him neutered. Surgery will limit the physical and emotional disorders that an intact cat is prone to develop. Why wait for your cat to develop a disorder to heed this message?

12.

RELATIONSHIPS

"Kamere was a different cat before Coppy came into her life," said Sandy. "Unless I played with her or she was in my lap, she was bored and lonely."

Sandy told me this as I wrote down some further instructions concerning her cat, Coppy, who had a terrific relationship with Kamere, but was shy of people. Sandy had followed my recommendations for "socializing" Coppy and, so far, Coppy's progress was terrific. She'd become so brave she even ventured out into the hall—up until then, she'd been strictly a closet cat.

Sandy continued to tell me that she'd read what I'd written about the "single cat syndrome" in my first book, and that she was so happy she'd adopted Coppy for Kamere.

Yes, Coppy was Kamere's answer to the end of boredom and frustration. It's not uncommon for single cats to be unhappy; their behavior displays distinct symptoms of the "single cat syndrome." A cat who's the victim of the single cat syndrome suffers from the frustration of feeling neglected and lonely. If there isn't a way to release this pent-up energy, it's usually channeled into destructive behavior. The source of anxiety that causes mischief and destructive behavior is the need to be noticed.

This applies especially to an indoor cat who can't go outdoors and work off his energy. His energy level builds, his body becomes tense and tight, and he's a vulnerable target for physical disorders that may range from skin to urinary problems. Since he can't relieve his anxiety constructively, when it becomes overwhelming it can cause anxiety attacks, in which the cat becomes aggressive and hostile toward people. Even if their person yells at them, negative attention is better than no attention to them.

Chelsea was a young cat who suffered such a frustration crisis. Her boredom caused her to knock over whatever she could get her paws on and literally vandalize the kitchen while her people were at work. They loved Chelsea—but not her vigilante tactics.

Chelsea's problem was the single-cat syndrome, and the best treatment was her own adopted cat or kitten. I gave her people the instructions they'd need for introducing a new cat and encouraged them to act soon, before Chelsea added new material to her repertoire. Chelsea's people followed my treatment plan and adopted Tigger, a young male kitten. Now Chelsea's time is divided between herself and Tigger. No more vigilante tactics, because now she has Tigger to inspire her and keep her occupied. She can share her complaints with him and work her energy out in cat play instead of "horse play."

Mookey is a young, altered male whose late-night destruction derbys and early-morning serenades almost drove his person, Sally, cuckoo. She couldn't put together why he was such a torment. After I'd taken his case history and observed his outgoing personality, I could understand why Mookey was so frustrated.

Sally had adopted Mookey a few months before. Because of her acting lessons and work schedule, Mookey was alone most of the day. A neighbor's cat had stayed with Mookey for a few days, but Mookey's outrageous behavior increased after the cat returned home. Since then, Sally's boyfriend had moved in and Mookey became unbearable.

I explained to Sally that Mookey was bored, lonely, and jealous. Because of her heavy work schedule, he felt (and was somewhat) neglected. The departure of the visiting cat only increased his anxiety level. He had had a little taste of companionship and then poof—no more. Now that Sally's boyfriend moved in, Mookey resented the fact that he had to share even more the little of Sally's attention that he got.

133

Sally mentioned that her boyfriend liked and played with Mookey, but Mookey wasn't always receptive. I told Sally that Mookey was still threatened by her boyfriend and it would take a little while for him to realize that he now had another friend. However, Mookey badly needed his own cat companion. Another cat would fill his need to be noticed, dissipate his anxiety, and provide a constructive release for his pent-up energy. A companion would supply the recognition and attention that Mookey desperately needed.

Several weeks later I ran into Sally at a nearby deli, and she told me that Mookey had a new kitten, and that he was a transformed cat.

Some people adopt cat companions for their cat without experiencing any serious problems. Other people encounter problems between the first and second cats that are never resolved.

Tabby was a fourteen-year-old, spayed cat who never fully accepted her companions, Patchy and Jibby. Until they arrived, Tabby was the only cat. She was the center of attention. Patchy was adopted when Tabby was ten years old, and Jibby arrived three years later. Patchy and Jibby were both kittens when they were introduced to Tabby. Tabby's family made the common mistake of showering the kittens with attention and pushing Tabby to the side. This neglect caused Tabby to reject each kitten because they were now her rivals, instead of her friends. Although Tabby now tolerates them, she keeps to herself and only seeks her people for love and affection. Because Patchy is a more mellow cat than Tabby and not as set in her ways, Patchy eventually befriended Jibby and the two of them have a positive relationship.

I can easily empathize with the common mistakes people make in introducing cats to each other. Sam was originally my first husband's cat; I'd given him Sam before we were married. At that time Oliver was my only cat and he spent most of his time outdoors. He was the hit of West Tenth Street. His passageway to the great outdoors was through my front window which led

to the stoop of the building. My marriage and move to an apartment on the fifth floor of a building ended Oliver's outdoor life and started his life with Sam. Oliver was three years old and Sam was two.

Unwittingly, I did everything I could to dampen their relationship. I tried to push them together and yelled at Oliver if he struck out at Sam. The more attention I gave Sam, the more alienated Oliver became. It didn't occur to me then that Oliver needed my support and that my husband could comfort Sam. Oliver was more introverted than Sam and Sam's high energy level and ornery ways were hardly endearing to Oliver. Poor Oliver gave up the perils of the street only to meet the perils of

Sam. Eventually, Oliver and Sam worked out a tolerable relationship. Five years later Oliver passed on.

I have to admit that Sam didn't display any visible grief over the loss of Oliver. By then Sam was seven, and we were living with Paul. I decided that Sam needed a friend, but this time I felt I had learned enough to start him out on the new relationship in a positive manner.

Because Sam is such a high-energy cat, I knew I had to match his strong personality with a cat that could keep up with him but wouldn't be a threat. A kitten was the best choice for Sam. A kitten would keep after Sam until Sam accepted him, whereas an older cat would not be so accommodating. Sam's personality was hardly mellow so he needed no hurdles or challenges from another cat.

I first introduced him to a female kitten named Hobbit. But somehow she wasn't the one. Maybe Sam felt she was too pretty for him. Our friend, Geoff, had been looking for a companion for his cat, Schroeder, who was Sam's age but had a sterling disposition; so Hobbit moved in with them and Schroeder fell rapidly in love with her.

A three-month-old black-and-white male was Sam's next encounter. I named this kitten Muggsy because he came on like

such a thug. Muggsy took one look at Sam and puffed his body up to where he looked like he'd explode at any moment. But instead, he sauntered over to Sam and hissed at him. Surprisingly, Sam gave Muggsy a casual look and nonchalantly began to wash himself. When Muggsy couldn't get Sam's attention and realized that Sam wasn't going to hurt him, he kept coming after Sam so he'd be noticed.

What finally caught Sam's attention was Muggsy's tail fetish. Sam's tail is often in motion, especially if there's a source of unrest, agitation, or high energy around. With Muggsy's high energy, Sam's tail was in constant motion, and Muggsy was in constant motion, too, batting away at Sam's tail. I knew if I sat and watched them, Sam would pick up my anxiety and let Muggsy have it. So I disappeared into the bedroom to let them interact alone. There was no way I could force their relationship to work. The best I could do was to let *them* work it out and remain the neutral bystander.

When I returned to the living room, I was overwhelmed! Muggsy and Sam were together in Sam's basket. Sam had Muggsy pinned down and was furiously washing away at Muggsy's ears. I wanted to run over and kiss and hug Sam, but I knew I couldn't. If I did, he would get upset by my commotion and wander off.

During this time, Paul and I were often tempted to pick Muggsy up and play with him—he was so cute—but we knew this would only cause Sam to feel neglected and avoid him. Even though Sam had made the initial breakthrough with Muggsy, his positive behavior wouldn't be reinforced if we showed Muggsy any attention. Any praise we gave Muggsy had to go through Sam. This way, if Sam's name was mentioned in relation to whatever we said about Muggsy, he would feel included and responsive. When I told Muggsy he was a handsome kitten, I said he was Sam's handsome kitten and he was handsome because of Sam. Naturally, Sam didn't exactly understand the meaning of my words, but since his name was mentioned and I directed my energy toward him, he showed no animosity toward Muggsy. Over and over, I told Sam he made a fine choice when he picked out Muggsy.

After two weeks, they slept, ate, and washed together. I had a couple of rough moments when I saw Sam wrestling with Muggsy. Logically, I knew Sam wouldn't hurt him because an older cat won't hurt a kitten. (Exceptions include a street tom who might attack a kitten who competed for food or a mother cat who might ignore or kill a sick kitten who was a danger to her or the rest of her litter.) But it still was overpowering to watch Sam go after Muggsy. However, Sam knew his own strength and didn't really take advantage of it, and even though he was almost three times the size of Muggsy, Sam allowed Muggsy to win a few skirmishes.

When cats roughhouse with each other, they keep their claws in, unless it's a serious brawl where they're out to attack and not play. A cat's skin is thicker than a person's and of course covered with fur; so one cat can nip another quite hard without causing any wounds.

I enjoyed watching as Muggsy began copycatting Sam's habits. He picked up Sam's way of scratching the scratching post, squeezed in on Sam's favorite spots, and even tried to flick his tail like Sam. How lucky he was to have Sam for his private tutor, and how lucky we were not to have to deal with Muggsy's education. Sam was the perfect headmaster.

Unfortunately, Sam didn't have his Muggsy very long; he disappeared a year later when we moved to Malibu. After weeks of painful, constant searching, we realized that Muggsy was gone for good. Sam and Paul and I grieved together. First Oliver and now Muggsy!

Without his Muggsy, Sam was lost. He cried and cried and couldn't bear to let us out of his sight. Shortly after, we returned to New York and presented Sam with another black-and-white kitten. We named him Muggsy-Baggins so Sam could have two cats in one. That was eight years ago. They were a perfect match then and today their relationship continues to grow and improve.

As we did with Sam, it's also important for you to match your cat's personality with the cat or kitten you adopt. This way, the relationship isn't started with built-in blocks. It would be a lot easier if your cat could venture out and find his own companion; but this is hardly realistic, so you have to make the match.

An older cat is frequently the best match for a kitten. Yarbles was a young female kitten whose person realized she needed a friend to keep her company and work out her energy. Because Yarbles's person didn't want to deal with raising another kitten, he adopted Gotham, a former resident cat. Gotham was the ideal match for Yarbles. He kept her in paw, she kept him going, and together they kept their person, David, entertained.

The introduction format I gave David for Yarbles and Gotham was unlike Sam's. Sam had to be the center of our attention because he was our first cat and he was the older cat. It's almost always the older cat that needs support until he accepts the kitten. For Yarbles and Gotham, I instructed David to concentrate on Gotham and devote his energy to him. Yarbles, at first, might be confused, but because she was a kitten, she was adaptable. She would seek Gotham out for attention when she realized David was less available. Even though Gotham was the newcomer, he needed David's support to accept Yarbles and not feel threatened by her.

I usually advise people who want a companion for their kitten to adopt an adolescent or older cat so their kitten will have a big cat to learn from. But some people prefer to start off with a kitten. Rusty was a kitten that lived with her person, Paulette. Paulette decided Rusty needed a friend and I recommended Eugene O'Neill, our resident cat at the time. O'Neill moved in, and he and Rusty hit it off immediately. But Paulette couldn't adjust to O'Neill—she just wanted another kitten! Although she realized the companion was meant for Rusty, she felt her lack of enthusiasm would eventually affect their relationship. So O'Neill once more rejoined The Practice and by the end of the week he'd moved in happily with his own new person. (Fortunately, O'Neill's visit with Rusty was so fleeting that their parting wasn't traumatic. It was just a stop along the way.) Paulette then presented Rusty with Cindy, a young kitten, who was there to stay.

Lizzie was another young kitten who needed a companion. Again, I recommended an older cat and, again, the cats were happy but Lizzie's person, Barbara, wanted another kitten experience. So the older cat moved on and Lizzie's new friend was a kitten named Abigail. Barbara also planned to adopt a young child and wanted my recommendations. I advised her to have the child feed the kittens so they would have a positive association with the child. Barbara frequently had children visit so the kittens would be used to the child's high energy level.

Sometimes people think their older cat will hurt a kitten. Puff was a mature, altered cat whose person adopted Penny, a young, female kitten. When she saw Puff grab Penny to wrestle, she panicked. She was sure Puff would flatten Penny, so she separated them and went off to work. When she put them together again, Puff was annoyed and rejected Penny. Their person was worried and upset when she contacted me. I assured her that Puff wouldn't eat Penny up. He knew just how much strength she could handle. I advised their person to put them together, ignore Penny, shower Puff with love and praise, and all would be well. A few days later, Puff and Penny were inseparable and their person was ecstatic. Now she doesn't get upset with their cat play. She realizes that they know how to talk to each other!

A young or mature cat with a mellow personality will usually accept another grown cat as a companion. Rapunzel was a spayed female who was lonesome for a friend after her companion, Dobie, passed on. Her person, Sally, felt that Bertrand Russell, who was two years old and a former resident, would catch Rapunzel's eye. So Bertie moved in with Rapunzel. The progress was slow, but Sally realized that while Rapunzel wanted to take her time, she'd accept Bertie as long as Sally didn't favor him or neglect Rapunzel.

Two weeks later Bertie scored! Sally came home and found the two cats nestled together on the sofa. Bertie's body heaved with purrs as Rapunzel washed him over. Rapunzel had indeed accepted Bertie as her man and this was her announcement.

A shy or strictly cat-oriented cat is a well-suited companion for a cat that's used to getting all the attention. Since the shy cat will naturally feel more comfortable in the presence of other cats, there's less chance of people interfering in the relationship.

Bogie was a three-year-old, altered male who developed a chronic vomiting problem. Its root appeared to be more emotional than medical. Although Bogie was very friendly, he was also nervous. I recommended that a companion might take his mind off himself and relieve his problems. Clara Bow, a former resident cat, was Bogie's treatment plan. She would hardly compete for Bogie's person's attention. She was untamed, several months old, and strictly untouchable. We managed to get her spayed with the help of a tranquilizer, and another tranquilizer was necessary to get her into a carrier and off to Bogie.

During Clara's first day, she managed to knock down and break valuable ornaments, run across her person Phyllis's back while she was in the shower, and chose the space behind the stove for her nesting place. A few days later, she moved behind the refrigerator. About this time she became aware of Bogie and started following him around. Clara was nonthreatening and Bogie didn't fight her off. How could he resist Clara, who was plainly enchanted with him? It wasn't until the two were clearly a duo that Clara even got around to accepting attention from Phyllis and her roommate. Gradually, Bogie's vomiting attacks decreased. Clara was the extreme example of a cat-oriented cat, but she was Bogie's source of relief.

Since cats are instinctively territorial, their reaction to a new arrival (unless they're used to many itinerant cats) is, if anything, anxious and suspicious. So when people tell me how they just can't keep the new kitten out of their lap and how lonely the kitten appears to be, I remind them that as long as *they* amuse the kitten, their cat won't. True, it's hard to resist an enchanting kitten, but you must do your best until your cat has befriended him. Only then is it your turn!

One day while I was eating lunch at Harvey's Chelsea Restaurant, Linda and Dick Harvey told me about their cat J.J.'s new kitten, Felix. They'd followed my introduction procedure and J.J., in his own inimitable, ornery way, had accepted Felix. They mentioned how he didn't have much choice because Felix constantly threw himself at J.J. Progress was great until they went away for a few days and a neighbor's child did their cat sitting. When they returned, J.J. and Felix were alienated. In fact, J.J. was totally furious. They spoke to the cat sitter and he told them he did exactly what he was told. But he'd misinterpreted their instructions. He'd *ignored* J.J. and played with Felix. It took a few days but with a lot of reinforced comforting and praise, J.J. forgave Felix and they caught J.J. washing at Felix's ears.

The following instructions will show you the "Wilbourn" way of introducing a new kitten into your household.

Introducing the Kitten

1. The kitten is for your cat. You don't want your cat to feel the kitten will deprive him of any attention. You can interact with the kitten after they've bonded but *always* continue to refer to it as your *cat's kitten.* Your cat needs to feel included and in control. Wait at least 10 days after the two have solidly bonded before you interact with the kitten. Playing together, grooming one another and looking relaxed are telltale signs of a bond. Until then, extra strokes and hugs for your cat are in order.

2. The morning or early afternoon is a prime introduction time. Select a time when you'll be in tip-top spirits.

3. For lunch or breakfast, treat yourself and your cat to your *choicest* foods.

4. An extra dish for the newcomer is essential, but a second litter box is optional.

5. Don't schedule any parties or major domestic changes or events for the next week.

The Kitten's Arrival

1. An escort is needed *only* to bring the kitten in. The escort should be someone your cat has not previously befriended. The escort should carry the kitten into the bathroom and open the lid of the carrier. (At this time you and your cat are closed in the bedroom with your cat's favorite things.) Before the escort departs, he or she should leave the bathroom door slightly ajar.

2. Open the bedroom door when you hear the escort leave so your cat, at will, can slip out and eventually discover its new friend. *But you should leave home and entertain yourself grandly for at least four or five hours.* Trust your cat to take care of itself and its new friend.

3. Upon your return, remember that the kitten is "invisible." It's important to pay zero attention to the kitten until two weeks after the two have bonded. If you interfere, the longer that will take. Be brave! The kitten will seek your cat out repeatedly if you ignore the kitten. You want to convey to your cat that it's your primary concern and the *kitten's* welfare is your cat's responsibility.

4. Tell your cat at feeding time that you've put down an extra dish so your cat's food is safe.

5. Now and *forever* when you do something for the kitten, mention your cat's name so that it feels included. It will become second nature to you.

Don't think your cat will be deceived if you sneak attention to the kitten on the *sly.* Your cat can't be fooled because a cat is a medium for fluctuations in energy and doesn't have to "see" because it can "feel" what's happening!

Important: Under normal circumstances a cat will not hurt a kitten, but the reaction of an intact male cat to a kitten can be dubious or an adverse reaction can occur if the kitten is ill. The older cat may attack the kitten out of anxiety or self-defense. *Relax* if the older cat hisses. Action speaks louder than hisses. Don't manipulate because a cat is repelled when you try. *

If you're introducing an older cat to your present cat, it may be best to start the newcomer with the aid of an escort in its own room so the cats can sniff but not confront each other for a few days. Later you can add a screen door for more contact. However, remember to dote on "your cat," etc. If your cat and the new cat are both very social, my kitten introduction may be appropriate. (In some situations, a tranquilizer is needed as auxiliary support to integrate the newcomer harmoniously.)

Key Reminders:

1. Your friends must also *ignore* the kitten and concentrate attention on your cat as above.

2. Don't permit the kitten in your bed if your cat sleeps elsewhere. Even if your cat *never* chose to sleep with you, it would be offended if the kitten did. If your cat sleeps with you and doesn't object to the kitten's presence in bed–fine! Trust that the kitten's psyche won't be damaged if you keep a low profile for awhile and your cat is in charge. Before long you'll have *two* dear friends and you'll be part of their purring.

Remember that a relationship takes time to construct, and they may not be "kissing kitties" in a few days. The more relaxed you remain the faster their relationship will develop. If they should ignore you, don't feel jealous; soon you'll have both of them seeking your lap. However, if within a few days

---

*If the newcomer is an older cat that is being introduced to a kitten, give the newcomer attention and refer to your kitten as the cat's friend. A kitten is more flexible and will seek out the newcomer for the attention it lacks from you.

your cat is going off by himself and his new kitten is in your lap, you're on the wrong track! Pay attention to your cat's message. He's trying to tell you that he *needs* you. Even if he appears to avoid you, seek him out and forget the kitten. They'll take forever to become good friends if you favor the kitten over the older cat.

If you have a younger brother or sister, maybe you remember, as I do, how you felt the first time you saw your parents touch your younger sibling. I was filled with ambivalent feelings. Yes, I wanted the baby to stop crying, but I felt that my parents should be touching *me*. It wasn't until my parents repeatedly reassured me and told me that they loved me and that the baby was going to be my friend that I began to accept my new sister. The more they tried to push me together with her, the more I withdrew and rejected her. I was suspicious of their motives–it had to be *my* decision to accept her. I wasn't having any baby forced on me!

Among our illustrious rank of residents at The Practice, we had several mama-kitten relationships. Each mama clearly communicated how she felt about her kids and which one, if any, she preferred. Katie Hepburn was an outrageous mama from the East Village. She stashed her kittens out on a client's fire escape. There were six of them and probably not all six were hers. Our client thought she'd gathered up other aban-

doned waifs because some kittens appeared older than the others, and it took her a few days to get them up the fire escape. She just kept showing up with more. Either Katie liked large families or she was the Major Barbara of the cat world, taking care of indigent kittens.

As it turned out, once Katie had deposited her kittens near cat-caring people, she made it clear that she'd done her part. Now it was up to her sponsors. Luckily, we knew of people who wanted kittens and managed to find them all homes.

Jean Darling was another mama cat. Lithe and beautiful, she supervised her kids, Alfalfa and Buckwheat, but preferred her privacy. She had no milk left to give them, but fortunately, they were old enough to eat on their own. Alfalfa was as shy and sensitive as Buckwheat was fierce and fast. While Buckwheat did cartwheels, Alfalfa preferred a lap. They interacted well together but weren't inseparable. Maybe they inherited their aloofness from their mama.

The "Our Gang" members each went off alone. They indicated no desire to remain together. Buckwheat joined Rosenante, a beautiful, older cat with numerous toes, and Alfalfa moved in with Curry, a debonaire redhead. Darling was whisked off to live on Long Island and joined an older kitten. Perhaps it's true that someone else's kids are often more appealing.

Alfalfa took a while to lose his shyness and Curry took the lead. However, two years later his people mentioned how lately he hung out in the window and purred away as passersby admired him. If Curry tried to join him, he'd reluctantly move a paw.

Buckwheat, who became D.Q., continues to live up to his fiery reputation but has mellowed a bit. Rosenante has her toes full!

Isadora Duncan was a mama who indeed loved her infants. Beautiful, but frail and worn-out after a bout with a severe upper respiratory virus, Isadora had little resources and milk; but she worked away at nurturing her little ones. With supplemental food and vitamins, Isadora and her infants, Nureyev,

Fonteyn, and Nijinsky, rallied. Although Isadora treated all her three kids tenderly and lovingly, it was Fonteyn, the little female, who clung to her. The two guys were more independent and preferred to go off by themselves.

When adoption time arrived, I made sure we carried out Isadora's wishes. Nureyev moved in with Sasha, a young Maltese kitten, who looked just like him. Nijinsky joined an older male who desperately needed a friend. But Isadora and Fonteyn went off together. Such an ending! They danced their way to happiness.

Lady Sophia Loren was a gorgeous looking mama. Of her three kittens, only one survived—T.J. There was no way we could separate them. Their fate was indeed to remain together; T.J. hung on Loren's every paw. They went to live with Shelley, whose cat, Ricky, had passed on. He'd been her only cat and this dazzling duo provided her with endless entertainment. Recently I spoke to Shelley and she mentioned how T.J. still follows Loren's lead. If she gave them a toy to play with or brought a box or bag into the house, it would be Loren who ventured forth. T.J. would wait until Loren checked things out or made the object available and only then would she respond. T.J. had chosen to remain her mother's daughter.

Mama Star is a snow-white cat. She was less than a year old when she produced five kittens, or Starlings, as I called them. Four of the Starlings were white females—Twinkle, Sparkle, Razzle, and Dazzle. It was hard to tell Twinkle from Dazzle, but Twinkle was the sleepiest. Sparkle was the cuddliest. Razzle enjoyed a good tussle and Dazzle never kept still. Babble was the little man in the family. He was white but had gray tiger thrown in—perhaps from his papa. We'd never know for sure.

The girls were true spitfires. The only way Mama Star had any peace was to climb to the top of the floor-to-ceiling scratching post. They couldn't make it up! From her perch Mama had a top-rate view. If one of the Starlings wandered too far or got into trouble, Mama would make a low but vibrant noise from her throat to her gut, and the Starling would take notice. If she didn't get any satisfaction, Mama would leave her post and take care of business.

Babble was delicate and dainty—unlike the girls, his energy was soft and low. Although he slept and played with the girls, he was a true mama's boy. He never got enough of her milk and he'd try to nurse her from whatever position she took. Perhaps because he was so gentle, Mama Star was patient with him. With a five to one ratio, maybe she sympathized with his sex! After all the other Starlings went off, Babble and Mama went off as a team to enjoy country life in Massachusetts.

It's not unusual for a female cat to mother her kittens for as long as she decides it's necessary, and then to seek her independence. Diamond Lil, a fluffy, long-haired number, appeared at The Practice with her son, Studs Lonigan. At least, they started off that way. But Lil soon sought Paul's desk as her own separate spot. At first Studs tried to accompany her but she ignored him. Fortunately, he wasn't put off and sprawled out every and anywhere. A few days later he moved in with Sinbad, a young, altered male. Diamond Lil was barely eight months old. Maybe Studs had blossomed in a moment of passion or her person wanted to have kittens around; but it was evident that Lil now chose to be a liberated ma. She would take care of herself, and someone else could show Studs the way.

People frequently wonder how their two cats who are littermates can be so different in disposition and personality. My experiences with these various kittens has demonstrated to me that a mother only partially contributes to her kitten's personalities, and that her personality is not necessarily the dominant or sole factor affecting her offspring's temperament.

Often people who have two cats consider adopting a third. I usually advise against it. Adding a third cat sets up a triangle and usually one cat is left by himself. I feel cats generally do better in pairs. However, there are exceptions.

Sneakers is a young, spayed female whose companion cat is

Ricky, a younger, altered male. Whereas Sneakers is retiring and demure, Ricky is a dynamo. He would prefer if Sneakers would play with him 'round-the-clock, but this isn't her idea of bliss. Their person, Norma, solved the dilemma. She introduced them to a neighbor's cat who makes a daily social call. His personality pleases Sneakers because he's mellow and nonthreatening. But best of all, he's Ricky's sort of guy. And while they frolic and gallivant, Sneakers has time for a leisurely wash and snooze.

Some cats share their home with a dog. Of these relationships, there are those in which the dog and cat respect each other but passion is on the minus side. Rousseau, a six-year-old, altered male cat has a companion, Riley, who's a five-year-old Irish setter. It was Rousseau's house first, so Riley, in spite of his size, had to swallow the reality that he had invaded Rousseau's territory. Thus, Rousseau was several whiskers in front to start. When Rousseau is pleased with Riley's manners, he'll seek him out. He especially prefers to be near Riley when he's stretched out on the rug with his huge front paws spread before him. At such times Rousseau curls himself into the crook of Riley's paws and his face fills with smiles. But most of the time Rousseau interacts with his people. Bedtime is when he feels most special —he gets to sleep in bed with his people, while Riley has to sleep on the rug.

Cary Grant, the Siamese warrior and his cat, Gable (whom I mentioned earlier), share their home with two other cats, Schwoogie and Rocky. But the extra added attraction is Ian, an energetic Siberian husky. Although Ian frequently manages to call the shots with Schwoogie and Rocky, who are easygoing, Lord Grant allows no such dog play either toward him or Clark. All Cary has to do is stare at Ian when he gets out of line and Ian moves on.

Sam, a mature, altered male, lives with a large shepherd dog who spends most of his time outdoors on a long, secured lead. Their relationship is "strictly for the cats" and Sam's the perpetual tease. He's figured out exactly how long the dog's lead extends and when Sam's looking for kicks, he'll park himself only a smidgen away from the end of the lead. Each time, the dog barks and carries on because Sam's there but out of reach; Sam plays possum and looks the other way as he lazily washes his paws. When the dog's on the loose, however, Sam takes a walk.

Mary, a friend of ours, lives on San Francisco's Telegraph Hill with her husband, cat Bleecker, and dog Petrouschka. Bleecker is a fluffy, altered male and Petrouschka is a sprawling, female Afghan who things she's Bleecker's size. Bleecker has a fuzzy, cat-shaped rug that is a comfortable size for a cat. Petrouschka feels that what's good for Bleecker has to be good for her; so whenever she's sleepy and the cat rug is vacant, she curls herself up as tiny as she can, and plants her giant body on the miniature mat. She usually does this when Bleecker is sitting before the picture window, eagerly awaiting Mary's arrival. When Mary's husband comes home he knows that Mary hasn't arrived yet if Bleecker is perched by the window and Petrouschka is on the cat mat. This situation strikes me as role exchanging: while Petrouschka plays cat, Bleecker takes on the role of man's best friend, impatiently anticipating his person's appearance.

Our guys are not avidly dog-oriented but they do tolerate our neighbors' dogs. Baggins, especially! When our next-door neighbor, Lillian, had her dog Cleo, Baggins used to play "visiting cat." He'd scratch at Lillian's door; she'd let him in; and from a neutral position he'd observe and study Cleo. Lillian always offered Baggins delectable tidbits, which made his visits even more inviting.

Samantha is another dog that lives down the hall. Her favorite pastime is to play "fetch it" with a rubber ball. As her person, Karen, throws the ball down the hall, Samantha takes off, and Baggins casually sits and stares. But if the ball should roll his way followed by Samantha, Baggins plays "guard the ball," and Samantha hesitantly keeps her distance until Karen can retrieve it. Baggins usually has the upper paw with Samantha but sometimes Samantha becomes brave enough to approach him, and then Baggins gracefully, but swiftly, backs out of her way.

Donald Jr. is a sassy, altered male whose companion is a high-spirited dog named Junior. They both get their kicks from engaging in games of one-upmanship. Junior camps himself in Donald's cat bed and Donald luxuriously stretches out in Junior's. When Junior refuses to let Donald into bed at night with their person, Sue, Donald perches himself on the shelf above Sue's head. Most of this activity takes place when Sue's around, which satisfies their need to be noticed. But Donald, every now and then, goes out of his way for Junior. Sue tells us that one night she had baked cupcakes and left them on the kitchen counter. Later she found Donald carefully knocking a cupcake off the counter to Junior, who waited with open mouth. The crumbs on the counter revealed Donald's own debauchery.

There are some cat and dog relationships in which size isn't the main deciding factor. Sadie-Mae-Love-Bug was a former resident cat who bedazzled everyone with her cute button face and petite body. A lover of people, she was a terror with other cats and thrived on keeping them in line. But her special subject was Thackeray, our dog in residence, who was twelve times her size. Thackeray was hyperexcitable and needed constant company and reassurance. Sadie was exactly what he needed. She ruled him with an iron paw, but he loved every minute of it. Ms. Love-Bug gave Thackeray the attention he sought and he satisfied her Napoleonic need for power. Each was a plus for the other's self-esteem. The odd couple divided when Sadie moved in with Floyd, a young, altered male who could deal with her dialogue, and Thackeray joined Pearl, a cat whose dog had disappeared.

It's apparent that a dog and cat are not natural enemies. However, they are affected by their environment. A cat may sometimes be victimized by a dog because of the dog's person.

Carmella was a young, spayed female who lived at a nearby restaurant. She was an ex-street cat and frequently strolled outside the restaurant. One evening during one of her outings, she was approached by a man with a bulldog (a fighting dog by instinct who's trained to fight bulls). Carmella instantly took off and would've made her escape, but the man dropped the dog's lead and cheered him on to her tracks. The dog managed to sink his teeth into her leg; but Carmella made it away with her life. If the man hadn't urged his dog on, there would not have been such a battle. Carmella no longer lives at the restaurant. Her people took her home where her companion is a dog—a dog of her own inclinations.

One evening at an off-Broadway theater I got into a conversation with a blind girl who was accompanied by her dog, Flicka. He was so loving and friendly that I couldn't stop petting him. The girl told me how he lived with her two cats, Trinket and Knick-Knack. When bedtime came, there were four in a bed. She mentioned that Trinket and Flicka shared a favorite game. Her friends told her that Trinket would approach Flicka and give him a tap with her paw. Flicka's mouth would open and encircle Trinket's head, but not for long. Trinket would then emerge with a soggy head. When she was ready for another go around, she'd give Flicka another tap and off they'd go. After she tired, she would take a walk.

If your cat has a happy relationship with his companion, you all will benefit.

13.

CATS' REACTIONS TO
THEIR PEOPLE'S FEELINGS
AND BODY LANGUAGE

I couldn't imagine how it would be not to have The Cat Practice. It was part of our lives for the past five years. But Paul and I had decided, for many reasons, that it was time to turn The Practice over to someone else and move on to other things. With these thoughts racing through my mind, I sat on the living room sofa and petted Sam and Baggins. They had just finished their evening meal and it was their time to be stroked and held until it was my time to write before I returned to The Practice.

Usually, after kneading out a cozy spot, Baggins plants himself on my chest and Sam jumps onto my legs. This time Baggins began his traditional knead, but stopped in the middle and wandered off to his basket in the bedroom. Sam poked up and down my body a few times and finally jumped down to the floor. I wondered why they were behaving differently; then Sam's next action gave me my answer. He sat before me and very deliberately licked away at his side with such gusto that he tore out little tufts of his fur. I reached over to pick him up but he ran across the room and resumed his trim. As I diverted Sam's attention with a serving of creamed corn, I realized why his fur had looked so peculiar during the past couple of weeks. We thought it was because Baggins was washing Sam's fur "against the grain." But no, it wasn't Baggins! Sam was responsible for his own peculiar look; suddenly I knew that Paul and I were at the root of Sam's discontent. For the past few months we'd been under unusual stress and unrest deciding what to do about The Practice. We tried to give the guys extra attention so they wouldn't be terribly affected by our tension, but they had been.

Sam trimmed away at his fur because his kidneys were acting up. They hurt him, and he was licking and trimming away in an effort to get to the source of his pain. (Sam has a chronic kidney problem, which is why his diet includes carbohydrates such as creamed corn and cream of chicken soup. With his moody appetite, we're grateful he eats them.) However, now we had to start him back on medication for a while, to give him extra support. I had arranged with Lydia and Elizabeth, a couple of teenagers, to visit and feed the cats on days I knew I'd be detained. But considering Sam's present condition, I realized that it would be best to have them come more often and, of course, that Paul and I had to be more available. Whatever our course of action concerning The Practice, it would be a while before our anxiety level would fall. In the meantime, our guys shouldn't have to suffer the consequences.

The next morning, Baggins strained in the litterbox without any success. Sam's stress targets are his mouth and kidneys but with Baggins, it's his bladder and anal glands. I didn't think he was obstructed and I knew Paul was in the midst of surgery at The Practice; so I gave him some catnip. This would help him to work out his energy so his body could relax. Baggins tore away at the catnip, rolled around the floor, enjoyed a peaceful high, and finally returned to the litterbox where he tinkled out a stream. Catnip for Baggins is a great relaxer.

I made sure that I gave them extra cuddling before I left for The Practice and repeatedly told them how much I loved them and how very handsome they were. Sam purred and soaked in the praise invisibly. But Baggins's reaction, as usual, was more demonstrative. As I repeated my talk about how pretty they were, Baggins stretched himself up and bumped his head against my leg. Saying the words pretty and handsome caused my body to relax and feel good, and my positive energy was transferred to the guys.

The mind, spirit, and body work as a team. If the mind is thinking unpleasant thoughts or the spirit is down, the body reflects the tension and contracts. If mind and spirit are relaxed and happy, the body expands and flows. Cats are very sensitive to sounds and body language because these are *their* primary means of communication.

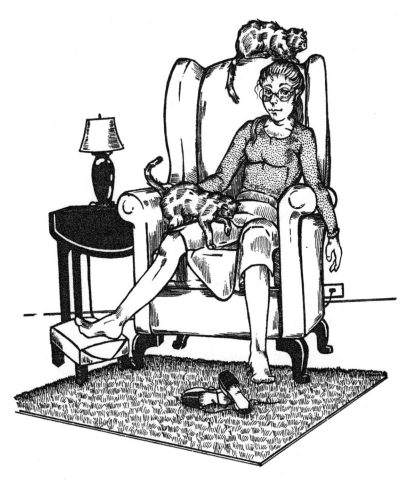

You may be surprised to know that a cat can be affected by his name. I feel it is best to give your cat a name with a positive connotation. This way whenever you call him or refer to him, the name has a positive association. If the name has a negative or neutral association, it may be revealed in your voice and body. Why pass on an unpleasant or negative feeling to your cat, when you can pass on a positive one?

Irene Adler is a young cat whose name is a perfect key to her personality (she's named after a Sherlock Holmes character). She loves to chase and retrieve a small rubber ball and prefers to have her person, Ed, play with her when he's in bed. If he doesn't respond to her first bounce, she keeps at it until he gives in. She'll appear suddenly at the sound of the word "ball" and will hide the ball for Ed to find it. If he won't, she'll bound off and return with it in her mouth. The great Holmes would be proud of his Irene!

Some cats can become very offended if you laugh at them. During an interview, a reporter from the *London Daily Examiner* told me about his cat, Rasputin. One day Rasputin, a bulky number, skidded off a bedside table during an attempt to make himself comfortable. Rasputin's expression was so comical that his person went into a fit of nonstop laughter. Much to his surprise, Rasputin's tail dropped, his body rippled, and he slumped off under the bed. Rasputin stayed under cover until he was coaxed out with a bit of shepherd's pie.

Poor Rasputin, his feelings were hurt! His person's laughter had injured his pride. The shepherd's pie was a delight, but the laughter was all wrong for a dignified cat.

A cat is very often affected by anxiety caused by separation from his person. If he has a close relationship with his person, the person's absence can affect his personality. Phelps was a mature, altered male cat who lived with his person, a writer who spent a lot of her time at home. Accordingly, he was used to a great deal of time and attention from his person. When she broke her arm and had to be hospitalized for several weeks, her neighbor took care of Phelps. When she returned from the hospital she had to treat her arm delicately, so she couldn't rough-house with Phelps the way she had before. Her sleeping habits changed and she started her mornings later, which meant Phelps ate his breakfast later. One day while she was petting him, Phelps suddenly nipped her. She didn't think much of the incident until one night she had trouble sleeping and Phelps, who'd been sleeping at the bottom of the bed, attacked her ankle. After two more similar attacks, she contacted me and we arranged a consultation.

Phelps was very sociable but I could see by the way he carried himself that he had a lot of energy, and when he couldn't work it off in play or exercise, it could turn destructive. I explained to his person that her time in the hospital triggered Phelps's anxiety. When she returned home and could no longer play with him the way she did before and her daily schedule changed, he became even more disoriented. He was confused and frustrated because of her changed behavior. If she petted him briskly, his excess pent-up energy caused him to become overstimulated. He attacked her in bed because her movement startled him and he overreacted.

Unless he could work off his pent-up energy constructively, Phelps's bizarre behavior would continue. I recommended that the best therapy would be an adopted kitten for Phelps to play with, but his person couldn't take on another cat. My other suggestions were catnip and elimination of any liver or tuna from the diet. Tuna and liver can aggravate skin sensitivity. I also suggested that she pet him gently so he wouldn't become overstimulated and that she invite a neighbor's child to visit and play with him each day. If he didn't calm down, I recommended that she start Phelps on a tranquilizer to relieve his anxiety until her activity level could increase. But first, she should have his chest x-rayed to rule out any problem that could be a contributing factor to his erratic behavior.

A week later, I paid another house call to Phelps and his person. This time a reporter and photographer from the *New York Post* were present. (The paper wanted a story on my work.)

157

Phelps was very accommodating and had a grand time with the catnip I brought along. He gave the photographer many captivating poses and thoroughly enjoyed being the center of attention. His person reported that he appeared more relaxed after my first visit. She felt the attention really upped his morale and she was sure that even today's visit would be a super morale builder.

Sometimes cats may experience short bouts of separation anxiety that can cause them to have temporary or permanent reactions. When some friends of ours had their apartment renovated, they had to move their cats, Geoffrey and Ernie, to a neighbor's place during the upheaval. But whenever they went over to visit their cats, they were given the cold shoulder, for as far as Geoffrey and Ernie were concerned, they were being exiled. Shortly after they returned home, the cats reverted to their old amicable ways. The castaway feeling was gone.

Shoshi is a lovely female who can't bear to be away from her person's voice. Jim has an answering machine attached to his phone with his recorded greeting for callers. One evening he returned home to find the tape all run out. Jim was even more surprised to find no messages when he played back the tape. He thought it odd that all of the callers were hang ups! This occurred once again, but the next time, he was able to solve the mystery. Shortly after leaving home, he returned to find Shoshi stretched out beside the machine listening to his voice. Shoshi discovered that with a swish of her paw, Jim could be with her while he was away. Jim was flattered with Shoshi's devotion, but wondered how he would receive his messages on days when Shoshi intercepted. I suggested that he tape the receiver down while he was out.

Maurice and Bernie were mature companion cats who had a dramatic reaction to their person's absence. Dan had been on tour promoting his current book and his girlfriend was taking care of them. By the time Dan returned, they were putting away twice as much food as usual and constantly yelling at him for more. Dan was even more astonished to find they were twice as affectionate as they normally were.

I explained to Dan that Maurice and Bernie's food debauchery was a reaction to his prolonged absence. They were victims of separation anxiety, and filling their stomachs relieved their anxiety. Their increased need for Dan's affection was to compensate for the time he'd been away. I also told Dan that their behavior was probably complicated by a built-up, delayed reaction to the loss of Ollie, Bernie's littermate, who had passed on a few months earlier. To make sure they didn't have any lurking medical problems, I recommended he schedule them for a physical. In the meantime, he should indulge their food craving— but most of all, coddle and cuddle them. As they felt more secure, their anxiety would decrease, and their food mania would slow down. Also, they wouldn't be as dependent on him to constantly prove he cared. Although absence makes the heart grow fonder, with Maurice and Bernie, absence did a double whammy on their tummies!

Marital splits can cause a cat's personality to change. My friend, Kay, mentioned that suddenly her cat, Cali, became a different female. Cali had always been very passive. Her companion cat, Max, took all the bows and all of the bed! But Cali had suddenly become more assertive. She carried herself with a more defined air and when bedtime arrived, she ignored Max's attempts to chase her off the bed. At first Max was confused by her change, but he quickly accepted it as part of the new Cali. Kay wondered what triggered the big change. It hadn't occurred to her that her recent separation could have affected Cali.

Before the separation, there was probably a great deal of tension and anxiety present in the household. Afterwards, the energy was more low key and Cali felt the change in Kay. This allowed her to relax and be more protective of what she wanted. Kay also mentioned that she'd been giving Cali more attention and that Cali's response was greater than ever before. Kay's change of status was a plus for Cali. However, I advised Kay to make sure she gave Max constant reassurance, so he wouldn't be threatened by Cali's new role. It wasn't easy to wake up and find that the cat he'd been living with for several years had become a liberated woman.

Mimsi and Jean-Arthur are companion cats who were outwardly affected by their people's changed domestic status. Mimsi had been adopted from a household of many cats, which made her quite independent; she was not overaffectionate. Jean-Arthur was more responsive to contact. Of the two, Mimsi was the leader; Jean looked up to her. When their people decided to separate and the Mrs. started a full-time job, the cats' personalities took on new dimensions. Mimsi became more affectionate; Jean became less dependent on Mimsi and even found new games to entertain herself. The people's release of their built-up anxiety and the changes in their lives brought out changes in Mimsi and Jean, who both had to adapt to the new living situation.

When a couple who has animals separates, the fate of the animals is usually a major consideration. If the animals are not very devoted to each other but each prefers an individual, it's better to have each go with his respective person and later adopt a new companion for each. But if the animals are very attached, the preferred solution would be for them to stay together. If they must be separated, each will need an abundant supply of love and comforting to compensate for the loss of his companion.

Sometimes the stress of separation can trigger a physical disorder. A few months after my separation from my first husband, my cat, Oliver, suffered a urinary attack. His primary stress target at the time was his bladder. At first, I didn't connect his attack as a reaction to my marital separation. But then I realized that physical as well as emotional disorders often take a while to manifest themselves. This often puzzles people because it's hard for them to grasp that something they did weeks ago may eventually affect their cat.

160

If your cat is affected by separation anxiety and you are aware of its effects, you can provide your cat with the extra care and support he needs to protect him from maximum stress. It's traumatic enough for a cat to endure the separation anxiety illustrated by the above situations. But when a cat is abandoned by his person, there's a total shock to his whole system. People find it hard enough to adjust to new environments without any sources of familiarity. Most cats are creatures of habit and are instinctively territorial. Casting them out into the unknown can be very threatening to them. You may have noticed how prudent and investigative your cat is when confronted with a new piece of furniture. He carefully checks it out before he takes it over. If you ever took him outdoors on his first outing, he probably crouched very close to the ground and walked very slowly and carefully, if at all. Or he might have hid under the nearest protection. Or, maybe he instantly retreated back to the door he came out. Imagine how frightened and bewildered he would be if one day you just offered him up to the street! If the cat's person abandons him to the streets, and even if the cat is lucky enough to be found and adopted immediately, the stress of the separation can trigger emotional and/or physical problems.

The exception might be an outdoor cat who prefers the street to living in a home. There are some cats that thrive on street living; they are true street urchins. But even among many of them, there are those that like to have a home to go to when they're in the mood for three "squares" or a comforting word.

An abandoned cat is often hit by a car in his frantic efforts to adapt to the street. Not every domesticated cat can adapt to street living. An extroverted, active house cat might fall to pieces in the street. Cars are not the only hazards. It is not unknown for children to mistreat wandering cats.

A cat on the loose often has a better chance of survival if he's wary of people, because not every person is a cat lover. Most street cats have this instinctive awareness, but domesticated cats are usually more people-oriented. It can be to their advantage if they approach a cat person who can offer them a home or who knows a friend who can. But sometimes they can come into contact with a foe instead of a friend.

There was an abandoned trio of whom I still have a vivid impression: Will Rogers, Billy Rose, and Lorenz were young cats that showed up at The Practice together. They were so petrified it took them several days to relax. Of the three, Billy was the most stunned and withdrawn. However, I noticed that Willy was Billy's security source. He followed Willy about and his body lost its tension when Willy washed him. Billy was the youngest and quite possibly he had received the most attention of the three from his former person; so he was also the most vulnerable.

It was obvious to me that Billy and Willy would have to be adopted together. Lorenz was the first to move on. I had hoped the other two would leave The Practice soon, because Billy, especially, couldn't deal with the stress of The Practice. Paul's relatives in California were the answer. They had a cat that needed emotional therapy. Billy and Willy flew out to live with them and their cat flew to New York to join The Practice. Several months later, his status was tip-top; he was adopted, and reports of Billy and Willy were glowing.

Sometimes an abandoned cat ends up in a shelter and many times, it's a one-way ticket. Even if he is adopted immediately, his stress tolerance has been heavily challenged by the nature of the environment, which is much like an orphanage. Nefertiti was a young, female cat adopted from a shelter. In some respects Nefertiti's role at the shelter was very special. Because she was a pedigreed cat and very beautiful, the staff hated to see her leave and kept her around. Finally, they allowed her to leave. She was adopted by one of our clients who brought her in to be spayed. She passed on shortly after the surgery. Her autopsy revealed she had a malignancy of the kidneys. There is evidence that indicates emotional stress is clearly linked with cancer susceptibility. Nefertiti's day-to-day environmental stress at the shelter took its toll before she got her special chance. This is not to say that every shelter resident cat is a bull's-eye for disaster, but their vulnerability is much higher.

Unfortunately, a person's life-style can change so drastically that he feels it impossible to keep his cat. Remember Ring Lardner, Lady Biltmore's old fling? After she gave him the shaft, he was adopted by one of our clients. All went well for Ring until his person's life took on other priorities, and once more, Ring returned to The Practice. This time he didn't have to deal with Lady B., but Tallulah Bankhead was our resident cat at the time, and she really gave Ring the business.

Ring was not in shape to deal with another tough female. Tallulah had lost part of her leg to an elevator, and although she was marvelous with people, she often transferred her leftover anxiety to other cats in the form of aggression. Ring was a perfect target for Tallulah. Since Ring was once an outdoor cat, we fixed up a cat door in the basement. But he had no desire to venture outdoors, or for that matter, upstairs to The Practice. He preferred the solitude and space that the basement offered because he did not have to cope with another cat, namely, Tallulah. The basement was far from finished or furnished, but to Ring, it was his sanctuary. If we tried to take him upstairs, he would tense up and retreat. But downstairs, given one pet, he would roll over so you could rub his tummy. I decided to let Ring have his choice of residence. As long as he was happy and secure, there was less chance of a recurring cystitis attack, if the damage hadn't already been done.

Ring resided in the basement until he met our friend, Sue. Her cat, Donald Sr., had recently passed on and she especially wanted another black-and-white cat for her dog, Junior. Sue walked into the basement; Ring rolled over on his back and Sue was smitten. She wanted him as soon as possible. This time we decided Ring should have a royal send-off; so we hired a limo, away they went, and Ring became a Donald Jr.

163

Ring's departure was a good omen for Tallulah. She went off to live with Mothball, a young, male kitten who could endure her dogma and give her a run for her chow.

It's not uncommon for two companion cats who've been abandoned by their person to transfer their aggression to each other. The Dolly Sisters had a thick and tight relationship until their person gave them up. The stress of the breakup caused Rosie Dolly to transfer her anxiety to Jenny Dolly. When Jenny tried to wash Rosie in her usual way and Rosie beat her up, she was totally disoriented. After repeated attempts, Jenny gave up, and each went their separate ways. Jenny moved in with Leila, a young, female kitten, and Rosie joined Smokey, a young, altered male who was used to a femme fatale. It's inevitable that some relationships can't be forever and it's easier all around if the parting is made as painless as possible.

On the happy side of the ledger, cats are tops at completing their people's enjoyment. Sam and Baggins have perfect timing when it comes to sharing our happy moments. Many evenings as Paul and I chat and relax on the sofa, our guys are right there with us. Sam usually sprawls out on Paul, and Baggins carefully kneads a spot on my body and settles himself in. Generally, they remain as long as we're relaxed. But if our discussion gets heated or our bodies tense, they usually drift off. If Sam's too worn out to move, he'll give a few flicks of his tail to show that he's annoyed and we should calm down. If we don't, he hisses and yells and moves to the other sofa or another room.

Paul and I are bran muffin fans and so is Sam. As we sit at the table and munch away at our muffins, Sam is right there waiting for his taste of butter and muffin. He feels that if muffins can make us happy, they're good enough for him. Baggins, food enthusiast that he is, is more of a meat and potatoes guy.

As I've mentioned, a cat is very sensitive to energy released by the body, whether person or animal. He doesn't rely solely on the five senses. If the energy is strong and positive enough, a cat will be drawn to it.

On many occasions while I'm happily cuddling one of the guys, the other arrives from the next room to join in on the action. If I haven't been talking, I know he has reacted to the release of positive energy from my body and his buddy's.

Sam is very responsive to cheerful and high-pitched tones. My voice can go very high, and on occasion, if I'm excited, it can be piercing. If I talk to Sam in a high-pitched voice, he responds to my "up" energy. The pitch of my voice has a quality that causes him to fix his attention. If he's in a talkative mood, he'll answer back. Neither one of us understands the other's vocabulary, but we do communicate.

Although a cat is drawn to positive energy, he withdraws from hostile energy. As for human depression or mournful energy, he is often attracted to it. A depressed person has a lowered energy level. His limp body attracts his cat because it's nonthreatening; cats often seem moved to comfort sad people. Duck is a young, female cat who, according to his person, David, generally sleeps at the foot of the bed. But when he's feeling depressed, she senses it, and sleeps by his head.

I can remember a night when I had a difficult time sleeping. My head was spinning, my body ached, and it was agony even to move. Despite my occasional trembling, Sam snuggled against my face and purred away. If a person is sobbing, his cat may try to comfort him to stop the noise. If the sobbing is loud, his cat will probably retreat.

Four months ago we sold The Practice. Since then, I've limited my patient consultations to house or telephone calls and letters; therefore, I've had more time to do my writing. Paul's new career has enabled him to have ample free time. So Sam and Baggins have us at home with them much more than before. They may miss their cat sitters, but it's given us greater time to spend with them and to be aware of their needs.

Sam has stopped trimming his fur and I've added new and tempting treats to his high-carbohydrate diet. Because we have to encourage Sam to eat more to keep his weight up and Baggins to eat less to keep his weight down, it's quite a balancing feat. To make sure that Baggins doesn't feel Sam is getting prime attention when we tempt him to eat, we distract Baggins with a walk in the hall. Fortunately, Baggins doesn't care for Sam's creamed corn, assorted veggies, or meat baby food. It's too weak for him!

Yes, Sam and Baggins have more time to let us know how they're feeling and what they need. In fact, right now Sam is in his basket screaming for me to bring him his midday snack of New England clam chowder. As for Baggins, he has started his soft shoe against the window. This is to announce that the pigeons are flying by and he'd like to join them. Guess I'd better go. My guys are calling to me.

INDEX

ABOUT THE AUTHOR

CAROLE C. WILBOURN is the first cat therapist and has been called "the founding mother of feline psychotherapy" by Mary Daniels, columnist for *The Chicago Tribune.* (Other descriptions include "the feline Freud" and "Jung at Heart.") In 1973, she co-founded the first hospital for cats in New York City. She writes a monthly column for *Cat Fancy* magazine, has a national house call practice, does international phone-and-letter consultations and sees patients and gives consultations at West Side Veterinary Center. She has recently introduced her first instructional audio therapy tape for cats and teaches classes for The Learning Annex. Look for her column "Dear T'abbe" in their magazine. She is on the advisory committee for The Humane Society of New York and makes numerous television and radio appearances. Carole Wilbourn lives with her two cats Sunny-Blue and Ziggy-Star-Dust in Manhattan's West Village.